To

_____

From

_____

On this date

_____

PRAYERS & PROMISES
for the GRADUATE

Pamela McQuade

BARBOUR
PUBLISHING

Contents

FOREWORD

You've just graduated—congratulations! There's a world of opportunity ahead of you in the great big twenty-first century.

As you build your future, make sure it's on the solid foundation of God's Word. That's the basis of *Prayers and Promises for the Graduate*. Each of these 180 carefully selected Bible verses is coupled with a contemporary prayer, making for very relevant, encouraging, and challenging reading.

We hope these "prayers and promises" will draw you closer to God and inspire your own prayers—and let you experience the truth of God's promise to Jeremiah: " 'Call to me and I will answer you and tell you great and unsearchable things you do not know' " (Jeremiah 33:3).

The Publishers

RIGHTEOUSNESS AND ANGER

For man's anger does not
bring about the righteous life that God desires.

JAMES 1:20

Could You make it clearer, Lord? I don't think so: When I am angry, I'm not righteous. No matter how hard I try, I can't make anger do Your will, because it's against everything You stand for.

So help me, instead, to control my emotions. When I see a wrong done, I know You don't want me to ignore it, but You want me to handle it calmly and in faith that You can work even in this. I need self-control to hold on to that truth when my emotions run high.

Even when the fire of anger licks at my soul, I want to remain strong in You. Let my responses always reflect Your desires, not my own.

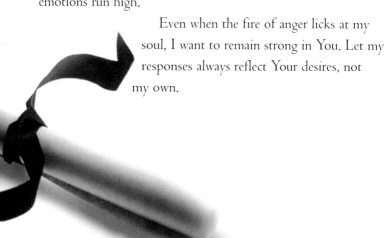

FORGIVENESS

*"The LORD is slow to anger, abounding in love
and forgiving sin and rebellion."*

When I've done wrong, Lord, I'm so glad You've promised to be slow to anger and quick to forgive. Thank You for not taking out Your anger on me.

But when I have to forgive someone else, I really appreciate what it took for You to forgive me. I begin to doubt I can pardon the one who's caused that hurt. On my own, I could never express Your forgiveness, because it just isn't in my dark heart. Thank You for giving me a new heart—one reflecting Yours—that responds with forgiveness as Your Spirit infiltrates every corner.

To be like You, I need Your Spirit's filling. Come into my spirit today and erase the anger that gets in the way of my being just like You.

GOD'S MERCY

The LORD is merciful and gracious;
he is slow to get angry and full of unfailing love.
He will not constantly accuse us,
nor remain angry forever.

PSALM 103:8−9 NLT

When it comes to anger, I can learn a lot from You, Lord. You don't get angry at the little things, and when You do get angry, You don't hold on to that emotion forever.

Sometimes, Lord, when I feel furious, I need an immediate solution. Something has gone seriously wrong, and I need to confront a friend or a family member. Not doing so could harm my life. Help me to approach that person with mercy and love. I want to deal with the problem, not let it separate our lives.

"Forever anger" has no place in heaven, so keep me from giving it a place in my life on earth. Help me be more like You, Lord.

A SOFT ANSWER

A soft answer turns away wrath,
but a harsh word stirs up anger.

PROVERBS 15:1 NKJV

When someone says words that hurt, I usually want to cause pain in return. But Your Word tells me that's not the right response, even if it is my first thought. My harsh anger does not benefit me or the other person. Instead, we'll end up in a circle of wrath that will last as long as our hard words and painful memories remain.

I don't want to live that way, Lord. Instead, I'd like to have Your peace in every corner of my life. So when that harsh answer leaps to my mind, help me bite my tongue. Please give me soft, appealing words that will ease the situation instead of escalating it.

FRIENDSHIP

Blessed is the man who walks not in the counsel of the ungodly, nor stands in the path of sinners, nor sits in the seat of the scornful.

PSALM 1:1 NKJV

I'm so glad You want to bless me, Lord. Thank You for letting me know that the people I hang around with can be part of that blessing. But I have to do my part by getting close to those who love You and also want to show that love in their lives.

Keep me, Lord, from looking to unbelievers for advice on how to live. I know they are missing out on so much because they don't know You. If living their way means hurting or giving up my best friend— Jesus—I want to run away from that lifestyle.

Let all my friendships glorify You, Jesus, and let that way of life draw others to You, too.

PEACE

The LORD gives his people strength.
The LORD blesses them with peace.

PSALM 29:11 NLT

Without You, Lord, my life would be misery. I'd experience a life of turmoil and doubt and be surrounded by confusion instead of Your strength and peace that passes understanding. But because of Your salvation, my soul is calm, and I feel confidence concerning my past and future. Your peace blesses all areas of my life—the days gone by, the present, and my years ahead, including eternity. No portion of my life has gone untouched by Your power.

Thank You, Lord, for Your strength for a new life and the blessings of Your peace that entirely recreate me. Your rewards for faith are more than I can imagine.

FORGIVEN SIN

Oh, what joy for those whose rebellion is forgiven,
whose sin is put out of sight!

PSALM 32:1 NLT

Hallelujah! You have forgiven my sin, Lord. Though I couldn't do a thing about my own wrongdoing, through Your Son, You destroyed all the iniquity that lay between us. Because of Jesus' sacrifice, that gift of forgiveness constantly fills my heart. His love made me able to know You and spend eternity with You.

How amazed I am that You loved me enough, Jesus, to put my sin out of Your sight. I, who had nothing to offer but rebellion, have been entirely forgiven. Though I give You my whole life, I cannot repay all You've done for me. Still I am thankful, Lord. Help me to show you that by a life that serves only You.

SPIRITUAL HUNGER

*"Blessed are those who hunger and
thirst for righteousness, for they will be filled."*

MATTHEW 5:6

If You hadn't told me so, I wouldn't think of spiritual hunger as a blessing, Lord. My goal is always to be filled entirely with You. Maybe I've been greedy about wanting only the best spiritual experience.

When a dry spell hits, I wonder what I've done wrong. I don't feel at all blessed, but hungry and thirsty for a taste of Your love. How glad I am that I can trust that even when I feel empty, You remain with me. In an unexpected way, You are preparing to fill me with even more righteousness.

I want to be filled with You, Lord, no matter how You do it. Fill my hungry soul any way You want to.

LIFE AND DOCTRINE

Watch your life and doctrine closely.
Persevere in them, because if you do,
you will save both yourself and your hearers.

1 TIMOTHY 4:16

Thank You, Lord, for giving me good leaders whose lives and teaching have been my example. Not only have I benefited from their lives, but in me they can see Your fulfillment of this promise.

I know it isn't always easy to be a leader, especially a Christian one. Help me to remember my pastor and other leaders regularly in prayer. Give them the strength, Lord, to remain faithful to You no matter what challenges or temptations they face. May they remain strong in the teachings of Your Word.

These leaders have blessed my life, Lord. Now help me to use what they've taught me to reach out to others, too.

A HUMBLE SPIRIT

The humble He guides in justice,
and the humble He teaches His way.

PSALM 25:9 NKJV

Lord, I thank You for those humble teachers who have been less concerned about themselves than about sharing Your truths with me. Though I haven't often given them praise, I appreciate the changes they've started in my life. I've seen You most clearly in those who have put Your glory before their own.

Keep my pastor, Bible teacher, and the other church leaders so in touch with You that they won't seek to make a name for themselves. Give them humble spirits that delight in drawing closer to You and sharing their knowledge of Your way with others.

Lord, also give me a humble spirit. I, too, want to know Your justice and learn more of Your way.

HEALING

Is anyone among you sick?
Let him call for the elders of the church,
and let them pray over him,
anointing him with oil in the name of the Lord.
And the prayer of faith will save the sick,
and the Lord will raise him up.
And if he has committed sins,
he will be forgiven.

JAMES 5:14—15 NKJV

When I'm sick, Lord, I run to the doctor. But you tell me that's not my only option. Not only should I come to You for healing, but I can ask my church leaders for prayer. Their faithful intercession has a powerful impact on both physical and spiritual health. They not only care about my body, but they recognize the importance of my soul's well-being to my whole life.

Thank You for caring leaders who feel concern about every part of me. Bless them today, Lord.

RESPECTING LEADERS

And He Himself gave some to be apostles,
some prophets, some evangelists,
and some pastors and teachers.

EPHESIANS 4:11 NKJV

When I disagree with a faithful leader, I don't want to jump to conclusions, Lord. Help me speak graciously.

No real Christian leader takes on authority without Your gifting and blessing. You've put Your people where they can serve You best, and I need to respect that. Instead of criticizing, help me be faithful in prayer for my church leaders, to lift them up so they follow You closely. Their hard jobs stretch their faith every day, and they need more support than critique.

I know You've given these leaders as examples for me, to help me understand Your will. Help me to appreciate their lives and testimonies.

A FAMILY

*"For whoever does the will of
My Father in heaven is
My brother and sister and mother!"*

MATTHEW 12:50 AMP

How amazing to think that You gave me a whole new family, Lord, when I didn't even think I needed one. But best of all, You gave me Yourself as an older brother, to guide me, watch out for me, and show me the best way to live.

I'm stunned to think You wanted me for Your sibling. How could You be proud of one who's so much smaller and weaker than You? Yet I am so thankful You chose me to live in Your eternal family.

Help me treat others in Your family as real brothers and sisters who share in You. I don't want any child in Your family to feel anything but loved.

SPIRITUALLY GIFTED

Now to each one the manifestation of
the Spirit is given for the common good.

1 CORINTHIANS 12:7

I know, Lord, I'm not the only Christian with spiritual gifts. You give them to each believer, and I need to recognize and respect the gifts of my brothers and sisters. Give me discernment and help me appreciate others' abilities so we can use them together for Your kingdom. We need to work together, not fight over who has the "best" gift.

Instead of becoming proud and self-righteous, I want to use my gifts to benefit my Christian family. Everything I do should benefit others, not just myself. So teach me how to use all You've given me to Your glory alone.

CHRIST'S BODY

Now you are the body of Christ,
and each one of you is a part of it.

1 CORINTHIANS 12:27

You promise us that as Christians we are part of Your body, Lord. That's something I have a hard time understanding. But I know it means each believer is so firmly connected that not one can be separated from You.

When I disagree with a brother or sister, help me to remember that. I can't pull a person out of Your body or deny the salvation You alone can give. Though I don't understand another Christian's purpose in Your kingdom, I don't have the right to deny what You have done.

Help me live graciously with other members of Your body, Jesus, because I don't want to hurt them or You.

BROTHERLY LOVE

He who loves his brother abides in the light,
and there is no cause for stumbling in him.

1 JOHN 2:10 NKJV

This commandment isn't an easy one, Father, but it comes with an attractive promise: If I love other Christians, I won't stumble in my Christian walk.

Love comes easily for me when I like another Christian. It's effortless to care for someone who shares my values and dreams or my likes and dislikes. Thank You for those "siblings" with whom I enjoy sharing Your love.

But You don't say I'll have a good Christian walk if I love a few like-minded believers. You want me to love every brother and sister. Help me love even difficult ones. Since only Your Spirit can make that possible, gracious Lord, please fill me now.

SELF-DISCIPLINE

For God did not give us a spirit of timidity,
but a spirit of power,
of love and of self-discipline.

2 TIMOTHY 1:7

As You grow my faith, Lord, You've made me aware that serving You shouldn't be a hit-or-miss thing—an option among others—but my life goal. Every choice I make should boldly work to forward Your kingdom, not my own self-interest.

I don't have to take that bold stance alone. Even when I lack strength to do the right thing, to make a choice that will be good for many days instead of just one, You help me decide well.

When I'd like to go for the short-term benefit, Your Spirit reminds me I'm not only living for today—there's eternity to consider.

In You I have a spirit of power, love, and the self-discipline that obedience requires. Help me to live faithfully only for You, Lord.

CORRECTION

Stern discipline awaits him who leaves the path;
he who hates correction will die.

PROVERBS 15:10

Lord, I don't enjoy being corrected, whether it comes from You or from another Christian. I'd rather believe I always do the right thing—but that isn't so. The truth is that to stay on Your narrow path, I need direction from You and wise believers.

Though I don't want to hear correcting words or experience those hard-hitting moments when I know I'm wrong, I know I need them. They seem unpleasant now, but they keep me from falling into greater error and missing Your way entirely.

Help my spirit to be gentle enough to accept correction, even when it hurts. I know You only mean it for my benefit. And if I have to correct another Christian, let it be with a kind and righteous spirit.

SELF-CONTROL

*A person without self-control is
as defenseless as a city
with broken-down walls.*

PROVERBS 25:28 NLT

Though self-control doesn't seem very appealing, Lord, You promise that the person who lacks it will be like an unwalled city, defenseless in the face of opposition. So many things attack me in my spiritual life that I don't want to forgo any defense.

Though controlling my tongue when I'd rather speak my mind, or doing the right thing when a sin is tempting, may not thrill me, Your Word shows me it's the only way to be secure in You. So give me the ability to bite my tongue or stand up for what's right, even if it isn't popular. Help me always to do Your will instead of what feels good today.

GODLINESS

Knowing God leads to self-control.
Self-control leads to patient endurance,
and patient endurance leads to godliness.

2 PETER 1:6 NLT

Just knowing You, Lord, leads to self-control. As I draw closer to You, I want to obey You more and more. Within me grows the discipline to do Your will and become more like You. As I grow in faith, without even paying attention to it, I start to gain discipline. It's one of Your wonderful benefits.

Thank You for not ending Your blessings there, though. Your Word promises that self-control increases endurance, and endurance leads to godliness. While I keep my eyes on You, You increase my faith in so many ways and provide all I need to draw nearer to You.

Thank You, Jesus, for Your many blessings, even the ones I wasn't looking for. You are a wonderful Lord.

GOOD DEEDS

In the same way, good deeds are obvious,
and even those that are not cannot be hidden.

1 TIMOTHY 5:25

Good deeds are things You want to be a way of life for each Christian, Lord. You've told us to do good and follow You. As I've grown in faith, good actions have become more natural. Sometimes I do them without thinking, simply because my lifestyle pleases You.

I don't try to shout my good deeds from the housetop. In fact, sometimes I'd rather not have anyone know that I'm doing them. Yet You promise that even those I don't want known will become apparent. Somehow, someone will realize that I've done good.

When that happens, I also want people to know why I did that deed. May it glorify You only, instead of gaining appreciation for me.

HEART'S DESIRES

Trust in the LORD, and do good;
dwell in the land, and feed on His faithfulness.
Delight yourself also in the LORD,
and He shall give you the desires of your heart.

PSALM 37:3—4 NKJV

What a generous Lord You are, Father God, wanting to give me my heart's desires. If I trust and obey You, live in a way that glorifies You, and put You first in my life, my life and heart become full. But whenever I'm less than devoted, no matter how much I receive, my heart remains empty. Only a life focused on You is perfectly blessed.

Though I seek my own desires, they always escape me. They're always one arm's length beyond my grasp—until I live in obedience to You. Then my elusive desires slip within reach because You've blessed my grasp. My desires become Yours, and suddenly I have them.

GOOD WORDS

*"A good man out of the good treasure
of his heart brings forth good;
and an evil man out of the evil treasure
of his heart brings forth evil.
For out of the abundance
of the heart his mouth speaks."*

LUKE 6:45 NKJV

How glad I am that You have made it impossible to completely hide either good or evil, Lord. When I need to assess someone's character, words help me see that person's heart.

But help me remember that other people also decide how trustworthy I am by the words I speak. My mouth shows my heart attitude. If I'm meditating on Your Word and following Your way, that comes through to You and others. If I've strayed, others know that, too. I can't always hide what's really in my heart.

Make me good through and through, Lord. I want my whole life to please You.

SHARING

And God will generously provide all you need.
Then you will always have everything you need
and plenty left over to share with others.

2 CORINTHIANS 9:8 NLT

Lord, You've given me so much. Thank You for the generous way You've cared for all my needs. Though I may not always have a lot of extra money in the bank, my true necessities are always covered. And I'm continually rich in Your blessings.

Whatever I do have, Lord, help me share abundantly with others. I know that when I give out of what You've blessed me with, You always replenish my store. Whether my need is cash, food, or a place to live, I can trust in Your faithfulness every day.

Thank You for being ever faithful, Father. Your generosity blesses my life.

AVOIDING DOUBT

Jesus replied, "I tell you the truth,
if you have faith and do not doubt,
not only can you do what was done to the fig tree,
but also you can say to this mountain,
'Go, throw yourself into the sea,'
and it will be done."

MATTHEW 21:21

It's hard for me to imagine this kind of faith, Lord. So often my own seems to get stuck under mountains instead of moving them. But I know that if You promise such things, they can happen.

Remove my doubt, O Lord. As I trust more fully in You, I know my faith will become strong enough to do Your will. That may not include mountain moving, but I know it can change lives, bring hope, and draw others to You.

Actually, you might call that moving a mountain, after all!

OBEDIENCE IN DOUBT

But the man who has doubts
is condemned if he eats,
because his eating is not from faith;
and everything that
does not come from faith is sin.

ROMANS 14:23

The situation Paul talks of here is so strange to me, Lord. I've never had to think about eating meat sacrificed to idols. But I've doubted other Christians' actions and wondered if I should go along with them. Their faith seemed so strong compared to mine.

Thank You, Lord, for telling me not to listen to other people, but to You. Listening to others would confuse me, but You always give me the right advice. It doesn't matter what others think of me, as long as I'm walking down the path You have designed for me. Keep me walking with You and listening to Your still, small voice.

STEADFAST FAITH

"Therefore I say to you,
whatever things you ask when you pray,
believe that you receive them,
and you will have them."

MARK 11:24 NKJV

I'm so glad that all I have to do is believe, and I can receive the best from Your hand, Lord. But sometimes that believing is harder than it sounds. So many things—even good ones—can slide between my belief and the words I speak. Doubts often come to me more easily than faith.

On my own, I'm not very good at trusting You when life turns black. I tend to forget this verse or doubt that it's really for me. That's when I need to realize that my eyes are on the wrong thing—this world—when they should be on You.

Keep me steadfastly looking at You, Lord. Then I'll have all I could ask for.

FAITH IN JESUS

"Blessed is the man who does not
fall away on account of me."

LUKE 7:23

S ome things You said, Jesus, present even believers with a challenge. I have to admit that you didn't make the Christian faith too easy. Sometimes I'm not comfortable with Your "hard sayings" because I don't understand them—or I don't like what they tell me to do.

But if I trust in You in spite of my lack of comfort or understanding, You promise I will be blessed. In my Christian walk I've already seen that obedience gets me further than qualms. Challenging doubt with faith brings a blessing, while settling for doubt just causes trouble. Help me stand up to doubts instead of giving in to them.

Thank You for that blessing, Lord. Keep me trusting in You.

HONORING PARENTS

"Honor your father and your mother,
as the LORD your God has commanded you,
that your days may be long,
and that it may be well with you in the land
which the LORD your God is giving you."

DEUTERONOMY 5:16 NKJV

Father God, I have to admit that honoring my parents isn't always easy. It's not that I don't love them, but we're so different. Still, the promise You gave is one I'd like to have. I'd like to live on my own turf, blessed by You. I'd like to have a long, fruitful life. So help me, Lord, to really honor my parents, and please help them to be good parents. I know You put us together for a reason; You didn't make a mistake. Help us discover all the wonderful things You have for us together.

GOD'S CHILDREN

*For his Holy Spirit speaks to us deep in our hearts
and tells us that we are God's children.*

ROMANS 8:16 NLT

No matter what happens to my family, Lord, Your Spirit has promised that I'm never alone. I'm always part of Your family, which may have members who get closer to my heart than some of my blood relatives. If I lost everyone You've given me—my parents, brothers, sisters, and my extended family—I'd never be alone. Thank You for caring so much for my heart that You bring me family members who love You, whether or not they're related by blood.

I'm glad to be part of Your family. Help me become a child You can be proud of, Lord.

WISE CHILD

A wise son brings joy to his father,
but a foolish son grief to his mother.

PROVERBS 10:1

There are lots of good reasons to be wise, Lord, but I really hadn't thought much of this one. I never thought much about how my wise or foolish choices affect my mom and dad.

I don't want to hurt them, Lord, and You know I haven't set out to do that. When we don't see eye to eye, help me understand what grieves them and how I can avoid any wrong-doing that causes them pain.

But even more than not hurting my parents, I want to please You, Father God. I want You to be able to point out Your wise child, who obeys You so well. If You are happy with my wisdom, I know my parents eventually will be, too.

GOD AS FATHER

A father of the fatherless,
a defender of widows,
is God in His holy habitation.

PSALM 68:5 NKJV

Lord, even if I don't have a dad or I don't see him, or if I just don't see eye to eye with him, it's great to know I still have a Father who cares: You. I know You can't come to ball games or take vacations with me in the way my earthly dad could, but he also can't do many of the things You do. Thank You for caring for my soul, looking out for my future, and loving me for eternity. I know that You know the future, heal all my spiritual hurts, and prepare me for Your kingdom.

Lord, no matter what kind of father I have, I still need You. Thanks for just being there for me.

RESPECTING GOD

"The LORD commanded us to obey
all these decrees and to fear the LORD our God,
so that we might always prosper
and be kept alive, as is the case today."

DEUTERONOMY 6:24

This verse tells me there's a right way to fear You, Lord. I need to hold You in awe and recognize the need to obey You. You are so glorious, so powerful, that to take You lightly would be foolish. It would even be easy to become terrified of You.

I don't go in terror of You because I've experienced Your forgiveness and love. But I can't make that an excuse for disobedience. If I don't obey Your will, I'll never have a spiritually profitable life. But as following You prospers me and keeps me alive, I know I'll be amazed at Your blessing on my life.

GOD'S PROTECTION

He will cover you with his feathers,
and under his wings you will find refuge;
his faithfulness will be your shield and rampart.
You will not fear the terror of night,
nor the arrow that flies by day.

PSALM 91:4–5

When You are protecting me, Lord, there's nothing I need to fear. Still, I have a hard time grasping such a weighty promise. Though my mind accepts it, it's so easy to believe otherwise when I face dangers in life. Before I even think about it, I find myself trusting in the things of this world for my protection. I look to friends, family, or government for safety instead of looking to You.

Remind me, when I face troubles, that I need only turn to You. Then, day or night, I'm perfectly safe.

LACKING NOTHING

Fear the LORD, you his saints,
for those who fear him lack nothing.

PSALM 34:9

L acking nothing: What a wonderful feeling that would be. I have to admit I often don't feel You've entirely fulfilled this promise in my life. Then I'm reminded of all the things You provide for me because I fear You: spiritual peace; enough money to cover my real needs, even if I don't get everything I want; people who love me; and a thousand other things I tend to take for granted.

Help me not to look at things I'd like to have and feel as if I'm missing out. They are really "extras" I can live comfortably without. You do provide me with all the things I really need.

As long as I fear You, Lord, I never need to fear the future.

EVIL AND FEAR

"Everyone who does evil hates the light,
and will not come into the light for fear
that his deeds will be exposed."

JOHN 3:20

Lord, I'm glad I don't have to worry about this negative promise. Because I've trusted completely in You, I never have to fear Your light. My life can be open to You, because You have cleansed my heart.

But those who are evil do fear Your light. They may try to envelop their sin in a haze of lies and prevarication, but they can't hide from You. Make me aware of those who love Your light and those who turn from it. I want to share Your light with those who need it and rejoice in the light with my brothers and sisters. Thank You, Lord, for Your light.

JESUS' REDEMPTION

In Him we have redemption through His blood,
the forgiveness of sins,
according to the riches of His grace.

EPHESIANS 1:7 NKJV

How glad I am, Lord, that my forgiveness doesn't depend on me, but on Your Son, Jesus. His grace gave me new life in You. When I could never have a perfect life on my own, and I desperately needed Your forgiveness, Jesus' blood bought my soul. His redemption made me new, from the inside out.

Help me live in Your redemption, Lord. I don't want to ignore Your great forgiveness or the change it's made in my life. Every good thing in me is there because of You.

I praise You, Lord!

SINS FORGIVEN

Though our hearts are filled with sins,
you forgive them all.
PSALM 65:3 NLT

So filled with sin is my heart, Lord, that it keeps spilling over, no matter how hard I try to contain it. I try to do right, yet I often find myself in the same old place, doing wrong. How glad I am that You forgive every sin. All I have to do is bring everything to You and ask You to make my heart right.

Now, cleanse me from the sins that have grabbed hold of me. Turn me back from wrongdoing and help me live in Your way. I can't do it without You, Jesus. I need Your Spirit at work in my heart today and every day of my life if I want my life to be a testimony to You. Take my heart and soul now, Lord.

GOD'S READY FORGIVENESS

O LORD, you are so good,
so ready to forgive,
so full of unfailing love
for all who ask your aid.

PSALM 86:5 NLT

How amazing, Lord, that all I have to do is repent, and Your love forgives my every wrong. Instead of holding my sins against me, You remove them far from me and even replace them with Your love.

I don't give others that kind of goodness, Lord. I often find it a struggle to forgive, especially when someone hurts me or someone I love. So fill me with Your forgiveness that I can forgive others, too. Make my life truly new, Lord, and change my hard heart into one just like Yours. Fill me with Your forgiving love and help me offer Your forgiveness to those who don't yet know You.

UNFORGIVEN BLASPHEMY

"Assuredly, I say to you,
all sins will be forgiven the sons of men,
and whatever blasphemies they may utter; but he who
blasphemes against the Holy Spirit never has forgiveness,
but is subject to eternal condemnation"—
because they said, "He has an unclean spirit."

MARK 3:28–30 NKJV

Every sin forgiven! What a wonderful promise, Jesus. Your people rejoice in that truth and see its results in their lives. Each day we bless You for the freedom You have given us.

But those who deny that Your message comes from God cannot experience forgiveness; their only "reward" is eternal condemnation. Though those who turn aside from redemption in You should never share Your kingdom, it bothers me that anyone might spend eternity in hell. So I ask You to open those unbelievers' hearts, Lord, to recognize their sin. Please use my testimony to show them the truth.

LOVE IN ADVERSITY

A friend loves at all times,
and a brother is born for adversity.

PROVERBS 17:17

L ord, anyone would treasure friends who loved no matter what happened. How rarely I've seen that kind of friendship, and how inadequately I've appreciated it in my own life.

Help me become the kind of friend who always loves, even when times are tough or things seem to be going against another. Keep me steady in caring, when others begin to walk away. I want to be there for my Christian brothers and sisters and show non-Christians how good Christian friendship is.

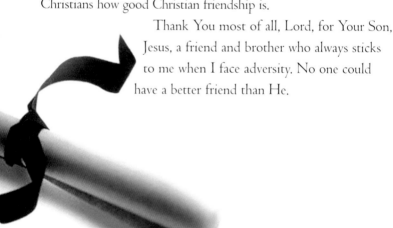

Thank You most of all, Lord, for Your Son, Jesus, a friend and brother who always sticks to me when I face adversity. No one could have a better friend than He.

Quality Friendship

A man of too many friends comes to ruin,
but there is a friend who sticks closer than a brother.

Too many friends" seems like a funny problem to have, Lord, but You're saying that many of these folks aren't really friends. Some people simply like to play at friendship when they can benefit from it.

Having a friend who sticks closer than a brother is wonderful, Lord. I know I always have Jesus, my best friend, but I also know what it's like to have Christians who've become so close they seem nearer than blood family. Your kingdom friendship, which lasts eternally, means more than a fair-weather friend or an uncaring sibling.

Help me stick closer than a brother to my Christian siblings. I know some have faithless brothers or sisters—and they may need to borrow one from Your family.

PRAYERS & PROMISES FOR THE GRADUATE   49

HURT BY A FRIEND

Wounds from a friend can be trusted,
but an enemy multiplies kisses.

PROVERBS 27:6

When a friend hurts me, it cuts deeply, Lord. But I'd rather hear the truth about myself from someone who loves me than listen to the lies of an enemy. People who hate me can't hurt me much, but they also can't help me by showing me places where I need to grow in You.

Open my heart to painful truths told by one who cares. Aid me in sifting what's said, to know which words are right and which might be off base, and help me forgive a friend who offers well-meant but mistaken critiques.

When a hurt comes directly from You, Lord, I want to be humble enough to accept it and profit from it. In the end, You are my best friend, who cares more than I can ever truly understand.

JESUS' FRIENDS

"You are my friends if you do what I command."

JOHN 15:14

Friendship with You, Lord, should mean the most to me. When I run out the door to be with another friend, I shouldn't leave You behind. Wherever we go, You can be a welcome third, who enjoys and blesses our fellowship.

Whatever I do, help me remember that Your friendship means more than any human relationship. I can't share with others the way I can with You; I'd never tell anyone else all the secrets of my heart. No one knows me as You do, even when I don't understand myself.

What You command, Lord, I want to do, whether I'm with others or alone. Help me and my friends to obey You always.

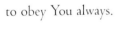

GOD~CAUSED FRUSTRATION

The eyes of the LORD keep watch over knowledge,
but he frustrates the words of the unfaithful.

PROVERBS 22:12

Lord, I've been frustrated by a lot of things in my life, but I'm glad that as long as I follow You, I won't be frustrated by You. I can't imagine the pain I would face should You be against me.

Because I know You, You share Your knowledge with me, teaching me how to live successfully in the world You created. Because You know everything about the earth and about me, You offer the guidance I need.

I can't imagine trying to live on my own, as one who doesn't know You. How painful life is for those who have never met You. Turn their pain to joy as they come to You in faith.

WRONG IDEAS

As the Scriptures say,
"I will destroy human wisdom and
discard their most brilliant ideas."

1 CORINTHIANS 1:19 NLT

You know how much we treasure our ideas, Lord. The things we think—the beliefs we hold—are precious to us. But You promise us that human ideas are limited, and even our most brilliant ones pale compared to Your power.

When other people's bright ideas would hurt me, I'm glad You're still in control. It's comforting to know that nothing gets past You or is beyond Your control. But help me to remember that Your power also limits my human wisdom. When I think I'm being the smartest, my idea is valueless if it doesn't side with Your wisdom.

Keep me in Your wise ways, Lord. I don't want my best ideas discarded because they are dead wrong.

GOD AS REFUGE

You evildoers frustrate the plans of the poor,
but the LORD is their refuge.

PSALM 14:6

If I had to choose between a wealthy evildoer and You, Lord, there would be no contest. Having You as a refuge is better by far. After all, a person with money has it only for this lifetime—but I can depend on You for eternity.

Remind me of that truth if I'm tempted to frustrate plans made by those who have less than I. Instead of choosing wrong, let me show Your refuge—and the unimportance of money in Your kingdom—to the person in need.

Thank You, Jesus, for being the refuge of all who believe in You.

CREATION'S FRUSTRATION

*For the creation was subjected to frustration. . .
in hope that the creation itself will be liberated
from its bondage to decay and brought into
the glorious freedom of the children of God.*

ROMANS 8:20–21

Y ou mean I'm not the only one who feels frustration,
Lord? It's simply part of living in this sinful world?
What a relief! Though I have to live with problems here
on earth, You've promised ultimate liberation. I can see victory
ahead, and I'm glad to know that when I reach heaven, no trouble
will bother me—for eternity.

You're even starting to free me from my frustration with sin
as I walk with You today. It's sort of practice for eternity, and I'm
glad to know what's coming.

PEACE

Mark the blameless man,
and observe the upright;
for the future of that man is peace.

PSALM 37:37 NKJV

Though this world sometimes becomes confused and confusing, I thank You, Lord, for promising me that if I live for You, I will have peace. In the middle of the confusion, I may not have all the answers, but I can relax and believe You are working. Trusting in You, I feel more and more peace inside.

I know it's only a matter of time before that peace affects the rest of my world. Help me share my faith testimony so others may also believe. When they come to You in faith, they can have peace throughout their days. And together we'll also share eternal peace with You.

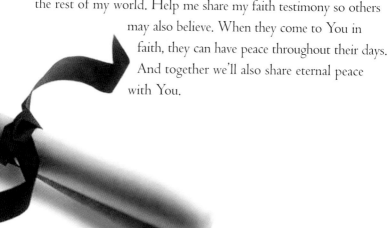

DESTRUCTION OF THE WICKED

For the evil man has no future hope,
and the lamp of the wicked will be snuffed out.

PROVERBS 24:20

Thank You, Lord, for saving me from this complete lack of a future. How empty life would be with no hope for eternity.

I know plenty of people who'd deny that there's hope for today, tomorrow, or eternity. If I look hard, their lives show it in their choices, their doubts, their speech, and their actions. Those attitudes make me sad, and I can't really change them, but I can still point the way to You. Give me the courage and the words to speak Your truth.

It hurts to think that friends, family, and other acquaintances could be snuffed out before they come to You. Help me to begin to pray for them all and be a witness who gives them hope.

God's Plans

*"For I know the plans
I have for you," says the LORD.
"They are plans for good and not for disaster,
to give you a future and a hope."*

Jeremiah 29:11 NLT

Even when I'm facing some terrible things in life, it's comforting to know You offer hope, Lord. Like the Israelites heading into exile, You promise me that the future is always bright in You. There are better times coming.

I can't see through my troubles today and into the future—maybe I wouldn't even want to, Lord. But I know You tell the truth when You hold out hope and a promise that all will be well. That's enough for me now!

GOD'S GLORY REVEALED

*I consider that our present sufferings are
not worth comparing with the glory
that will be revealed in us.*

ROMANS 8:18

What a vision for the future Paul had, Lord. Despite all his sufferings in bringing the gospel to the Gentiles—even to me—he knew his daily troubles were nothing compared to the glory You were working in him.

I, too, need a faith-filled vision for the future. On those boring, dark days, remind me of the glory You're preparing for me, both here on earth and in heaven. Though I can't see the end of Your plan, help me to trust that it will be more wonderful than I can imagine.

I know You want only good things for me, though I sometimes have a hard time believing that. Keep my heart strong for You, Jesus.

THE RETURN FOR GIVING

"Give, and it will be given to you.
They will pour into your lap a good measure—
pressed down, shaken together, and running over.
For by your standard of measure
it will be measured to you in return."

LUKE 6:38 NASB

I know people say no one can outgive You, Lord. My mind agrees when I don't have anything to offer. But when You ask for a sacrifice, whether it's time or money, I'm surprised at how easily I begin to wonder if it will be worth whatever I give up.

Forgive me, Lord, for hoarding the gifts You've given me. I know it's wrong, and I want to change my ways with the help of Your Spirit. Remind me that by giving generously, I'll be gaining in the end—in eternity, if not here on earth.

GENEROSITY

Remember this:
Whoever sows sparingly will also reap sparingly,
and whoever sows generously
will also reap generously.

2 CORINTHIANS 9:6

This verse reminds me that You give generously, Lord, and expect me to follow in Your footsteps. Because You've bestowed so much on me, I can share Your generosity. How will others know what You're really like if I hoard my experience with You, the gifts You've given me, and even the physical blessings You've allowed me to have?

Open my spirit to Your will, Lord, and help me give from a generous heart so I can experience Your joy in generosity. When I reach heaven, instead of a poor harvest that resulted from today's greed, I'd like to see a full field of good plants that took root in Your kingdom.

GIVING WHEN ASKED

"Give to the one who asks you,
and do not turn away from the one
who wants to borrow from you."

MATTHEW 5:42

When someone asks for my time or money, Lord, it's so easy to offer a quick "no" in response. How easily I object to people who want to take something from me.

Yet that person may not be taking something from me—maybe he or she is offering me an opportunity to be blessed. Whatever I give may be small in comparison to the blessing You offer in return. When someone comes to me asking for a gift or a loan, help me wisely discern if it's something that will glorify You. If it is, help me give as much as You have in mind, not simply a tiny portion that feels comfortable to me.

GOD'S GIVING

"But seek first his kingdom and his righteousness,
and all these things will be given to you as well."

MATTHEW 6:33

I'd like to have You give me all kinds of nice things in life, Lord. Good food and drink and nice clothes would be a good place to start. . .a nice place to live would be great. . . . Before long, I have a long list of wants.

But those aren't the things You really want me to desire. They're just the "extras." What You want me to seek first is Your kingdom and righteousness. You want me to want what You want and be what You are.

You give me so many good things, Lord. Help me to understand the source of every blessing and rejoice in You alone. Help me to live to rejoice in You—not the things You give.

GOD'S JUDGMENT

He will judge the world in righteousness;
He will execute judgment
for the peoples with equity.

PSALM 9:8 NASB

At times, I wonder if You really do rule the world, Lord. I see wicked people hurting the innocent and never seeming to pay a price. The world appears unfair, and no one corrects the inequity. It's hard not to get angry.

Don't let me forget, Lord, that You don't work on my schedule. Your own will be perfect. The timing will be just right, and the wicked will receive all they deserve. You'll help those who have been hurt and repay them a thousand times.

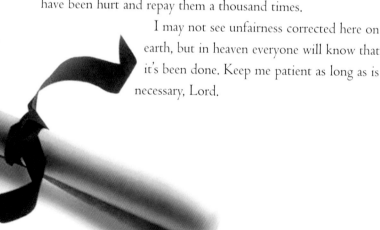

I may not see unfairness corrected here on earth, but in heaven everyone will know that it's been done. Keep me patient as long as is necessary, Lord.

GOD AS KING

The LORD is King forever and ever;
nations have perished from His land.

PSALM 10:16 NASB

We don't have a king in our country, Lord. Not too many nations have them anymore, so it's hard for me to imagine one person having complete authority over a country. But I know no human could rule so perfectly that I'd want him to be in charge forever.

It's not like that, though, when I think of You as King. Your rule over my life, Father, has made such a difference. I recognize how good Your authority is, and I wish that even now You ruled the whole world.

Still, I see You at work, bringing down wrongdoers and lifting up the faithful. You're still in charge even though Your complete rule isn't here yet. Let me be part of Your kingdom here on earth.

GOD OWNS ALL CREATION

The earth is the LORD's,
and all it contains, the world,
and those who dwell in it.

PSALM 24:1 NASB

Thank You, Lord, for controlling all creation, though things can seem so confused. I often wonder where this world is going, but I'm glad I can trust in Your control over all living things.

Even people, whom You created along with the birds, bees, and other creatures, are under Your control. Though they may not all glorify You with their lives, they cannot do anything to set aside Your command of creation. Their wickedness cannot destroy Your plans for Your world.

Thank You for owning me along with everything else. I'm incredibly glad to belong to the Lord of the universe.

ALL-POWERFUL GOD

Do you not know? Have you not heard?
The Everlasting God, the LORD,
the Creator of the ends of the earth
does not become weary or tired.
His understanding is inscrutable.

ISAIAH 40:28 NASB

It's so easy for me to become tired of this world, Lord. When sin weighs me down or I can't understand this planet I live on, the burden seems almost unbearable. How glad I am that You, my omnipotent, powerful God, never feel that way. There's nothing You can't understand or overcome. You never have to rest because You've faced something stronger than Yourself.

I'm glad I can trust in You, Lord, to reach even the ends of the earth with Your power and authority. You control all things, wicked and blessed, and bend them to Your will. Thank You for all You do for this world—and for me.

HIS PERFECT LAW

The law of the LORD is perfect,
reviving the soul.
The statutes of the LORD are trustworthy,
making wise the simple.

PSALM 19:7

Y ou have given me Your perfect commands, Lord.
Forgive me for sometimes trying to debate them with
You. Nothing You've told me to do is impossible—with
Your help—and it's all good for me. Your Word shows me
how to live and recreates my life.

It's hard for me to imagine being wise
under my own power, Lord. In fact,
I know it would never happen.
But as I follow Your commands, You
share Your wisdom. I become more and
more like You as I follow Your law.

Thank You for Your commandments,
Lord. Help me live them today.

BLESSINGS OF OBEDIENCE

"I have commanded you today to love
the LORD your God and to keep his commands, laws,
and regulations by walking in his ways.
If you do this,
you will live and become a great nation,
and the LORD your God will bless you
and the land you are about to enter and occupy."

DEUTERONOMY 30:16 NLT

You promised the ancient Israelites that if they obeyed Your commands they'd be part of a great, blessed nation, Lord. I'm no Israelite, yet I've seen Your blessing when I and my country have followed You. The old promise still works for those who love You.

I'm not only part of my country—I'm also part of Your eternal nation, Lord. No matter where I live, I look forward to the Promised Land, heaven, where I'll be blessed eternally.

Thank You, Father, for all Your blessings.

GOD'S DIRECTION

*"Anyone who breaks one of
the least of these commandments
and teaches others to do the same
will be called least in the kingdom of heaven,
but whoever practices and teaches
these commands will be called
great in the kingdom of heaven."*

MATTHEW 5:19

Y ou've given me a choice, Lord: to obey or break Your commandments. And you've told me the outcome of each.

Sometimes Your commandments aren't easy to understand, but I want to learn all about them and obey them more and more each day. You've given them to guide me in the right direction and keep me from messing up my life. Thank You for caring where I go and what I do, Father.

Help me to obey and pass on Your commands to others who also need Your direction in their lives. Without Your commands, we'd all be going in circles, Lord.

PROMISE OF GOOD THINGS

Hear now, O Israel, the decrees and laws
I am about to teach you.
Follow them so that you may live and may go in
and take possession of the land that the LORD,
the God of your fathers, is giving you.

DEUTERONOMY 4:1

It amazes me to think of all the good things that can be mine if I obey You, Lord. Over and over You've told Your people that anyone who obeys You will be richly blessed.

My land may not be ancient Israel, but I'm one of Your people. You have things You want to offer me if I do Your will. Whether or not I own a patch of turf here on earth, You have benefits for me both here and in eternity.

Thank You for being so generous, Lord, and for blessing my life in many ways. Help me obey You more and more each day.

COMPASSION AND JUSTICE

"The LORD, the LORD,
the compassionate and gracious God,
slow to anger, abounding in love and faithfulness,
maintaining love to thousands,
and forgiving wickedness, rebellion and sin.
Yet he does not leave the guilty unpunished."

EXODUS 34:6−7

How faithful You are to me, Lord, and to everyone else who trusts in You. Over and over I've seen You work mercifully in the lives of my Christian friends and fellow churchgoers. I see it in the lives of believers who share their faith publicly and in my own life, too. You never let us down, Lord, even when we go through trouble. You're patient and loving, forgiving our sins.

But You're also just and don't let the guilty—even Christians—get away with wrongdoing. Your justice is as perfect as Your love, Jesus. Thank You for that perfect balance.

COVENANT OF FAITH

Know therefore that the LORD your God is God;
he is the faithful God,
keeping his covenant of love to a
thousand generations of those who love him
and keep his commands.

DEUTERONOMY 7:9

Thank You, Lord, for promising Your faithfulness to all who love You and keep Your commands. Because I've seen Your faithfulness, the steadfast way You keep Your promises, I know I can trust You to do exactly what You've said.

You've promised to continue to love me; now help me to be faithful to You. I want to adore You, Lord, and keep the commandments You've given me for my own benefit. Help me to walk in Your ways and share Your love with my generation through a faithful testimony.

PROTECTION FROM EVIL

But the Lord is faithful,
and he will strengthen and
protect you from the evil one.

2 THESSALONIANS 3:3

When Satan attacks, Lord, I'm quickly aware of my own weakness. Though one minute I feel strong in You, in the next, the enemy's offensives suddenly threaten my faith. When evil pounds me, I thank You for offering me Your strength and protection. Without Your power, I'd be totally overwhelmed by the evil one.

Keep me from walking into Satan's traps, Lord. Protect me from unknowingly strolling down his ways. I don't want to get any closer to his dangers than I have to, and I won't if I'm walking close to Your side.

Today I need Your protection. You've promised to be there for me, and I need Your powerful defense now. Thank You, Lord.

FORGIVING SIN

If we confess our sins,
he is faithful and just
and will forgive us our sins
and purify us from all unrighteousness.

1 JOHN 1:9

What joy I feel when I think about Your faithfulness in forgiving my sin, Lord. All I have to do is ask, really meaning it, and my sin is gone.

But sometimes that's harder than it might seem. Sin can be so tempting, and it easily wraps itself around my heart. When I go to confess, something in me balks at the idea.

I want to live without sin and be cleansed from that deep-down evil that entraps me so quickly. Reach into my life, Lord, and turn my heart away from wrong. Through Your Spirit, divert my heart into right paths and forgive my every error.

Thank You for Your faithfulness, Lord, in making me like You.

GOD'S GUIDANCE

Your word is a lamp for my feet
and a light for my path.

PSALM 119:105 NLT

E very day I face challenging decisions of all sizes—
questions that make me wonder if I'm making good
choices. How often I wonder what I should do next,
Lord. If I look to the world for answers, I feel confused.
Everyone offers a different response, and after a while I'm not
sure who's right.

But when I turn to Your Word, I never need to
worry about that. You always give me good
advice, guidance I can count on.

Keep me daily in Your Word,
Lord, and once I know the right way,
help me to walk in it. I want to follow
Your light, Jesus, every day of my life.

EVERLASTING TRUTH

The grass withers, the flower fades,
but the word of our God stands forever.

ISAIAH 40:8 NASB

So much changes in life, Lord. Just when I think I'm secure, I can almost count on some fluctuation, and my world becomes different again. Just as the seasons alter and the flowers die off, life is constantly moving.

But Your truths aren't one thing in the summer season and another in fall. Your Word doesn't say one thing this month and something new ninety days later. It always shows me what You are like and never changes. I can count on scripture always to be truthful and to lead me in the right path.

Thank You, Lord, for sharing Your everlasting truth with me. Help me to be steadfast in clinging to Your way.

THE POWERFUL WORD

For the word of God is full of living power.
It is sharper than the sharpest knife,
cutting deep into our innermost thoughts and desires.
It exposes us for what we really are.

HEBREWS 4:12 NLT

I've known what it's like to be cut by Your Word, Lord, and I can't say I always like what I read. I'm pierced, as with a knife, when You point out my intentional sin or a place where I've failed. Sometimes I'd like to run away from the pain. But escape won't offer me a changed life. Only if I listen to and obey Your Word can its power heal my soul. Your truths change me and guide me in the best path.

I need Your Word's power to cleanse me from sin, Lord. Change my heart and give me new wisdom as the scriptures fill my head.

HIS PERFECT WORD

"As for God, his way is perfect;
the word of the LORD is flawless.
He is a shield for all who take refuge in him."

2 SAMUEL 22:31

I f I want to know just what You're like, Lord, I need only look in Your Book. The scriptures are perfect, just like You, and show me how to live a life that's faultless in You. With Your Book in my heart and mind, I grow in faith and Your grace. Without Your guidance and advice, I'll never become the person You designed me to be.

Thank You for writing down for me all Your commands and guidance so I can take constant refuge in Your truth. With it, You shield me from sin and give me grace to live well.

GOD'S JUSTICE

*"Have nothing to do with a false charge
and do not put an innocent or honest person
to death, for I will not acquit the guilty."*

EXODUS 23:7

When sin harms an innocent person, it's easy to wonder where You are, Lord. "Why did this happen?" I ask. "Why wasn't it stopped?"

Verses like this give me hope, though. You warn Your people not to do evil, because You will not acquit them. How much less will You acquit someone who has no regard for You or relationship with You.

When I can't see Your justice, help me still to trust in it. Let me know a response is on its way even if You don't show it before I meet with eternity.

FORGIVENESS

As far as the east is from the west,
so far has he removed
our transgressions from us.

PSALM 103:12

When I've done wrong, Jesus, guilt eats at my soul. Though I try to push it aside, from deep inside, it chews away at me.

I'm glad I don't have to live with those feelings every day of my life. Because You love me, Lord, You've offered forgiveness and separated me from my sin. You even promise to put sin so far away from me that no one—not even I—will be able to find it.

I still sin, Lord. When I do, draw me to Your forgiveness. Help me speak the words that admit my wrongs so I can again be close to You.

ACCOUNTABILITY FOR GUILT

"The soul who sins shall die.
The son shall not bear the guilt of the father,
nor the father bear the guilt of the son.
The righteousness of the righteous
shall be upon himself,
and the wickedness of the wicked
shall be upon himself."

 EZEKIEL 18:20 NKJV

My sins are my own, Lord, according to this promise. No one shares them with me, and I can't take on another's wrongdoing.

Though I'm glad You've told me this, sometimes I feel guilty for things others do wrong. When their wrong lifestyles impact my life, it's easy to get trapped, too, or think that somehow I'm responsible for their wickedness.

Help me to take responsibility for my own sin, but not the sins of others, Lord. I bring only my wrongdoing to You so You can cleanse my heart.

LAW BREAKING

And the person who keeps all of the laws
except one is as guilty as the person who
has broken all of God's laws.

JAMES 2:10 NLT

Even when I feel as if I do no wrong, Lord, my heart is not completely clean. If I followed Your Word and only made one mistake in my whole life, it would be enough to condemn me for eternity. Though I work at obeying You, spend time in scripture, and seek to do Your will, I'm still not anywhere near perfect. I can't even imagine making just one mistake!

Without Your Son's sacrifice, I'd be broken on Your Law, unable to approach Your holiness. But You provided this way for me to come to You with a broken spirit that recognized my sin. Thank You, Jesus, for covering my guilt and giving me love for You.

BLESSINGS

*Hear, O Israel, and be careful to obey so that
it may go well with you and that you may increase greatly
in a land flowing with milk and honey, just as the LORD,
the God of your fathers, promised you.*

DEUTERONOMY 6:3

Y ou promised the ancient Israelites that obeying You
would lead to the blessing of the Promised Land. They
could trust their Father to give them both physical and
spiritual benefits.

No less do You bless me, Lord, when I obey
You. I may not have a tract of turf in my
future, but You will provide for all my
needs, spiritual and physical.
When I trust in You, listen to Your
commands, and obey You, You provide
milk, honey, and a lot of other things.
Thank You, Lord, for all Your
blessings.

HUMBLE BEFORE GOD

*"If My people who are called by
My name will humble themselves,
and pray and seek My face,
and turn from their wicked ways,
then I will hear from heaven,
and will forgive their sin and heal their land."*

2 CHRONICLES 7:14 NKJV

Our land needs healing no less than the Israelites' did, but sometimes we find it hard to realize that, Lord. We've turned from You and replaced Your truths with our own ideas of goodness. Though our society suffers from that misplaced trust, we still have difficulty hearing Your truth.

Open my ears to Your words, Lord. Help me to see all I've done that has been outside Your will—and to ask Your forgiveness. When I'm walking in Your right path, I can reach out to my country, through word and deed.

GOD'S WARNING

"Hear, O my people,
and I will warn you—
if you would but listen to me,
O Israel!"

PSALM 81:8

None of us can complain that You have not warned us, Lord. You've given us Your Word, let us run ourselves into trouble, and shown us that our own solutions go nowhere. Yet even though the message sounds out loud and clear, we sometimes have a hard time heeding Your warning, Lord.

I want to pay attention to Your warnings, Lord, whether they come from Your Word, the results of a mistaken life choice, or another Christian. Help me discern what is of You and open my ears wide for Your words.

FOLLOWING GOD

"My sheep hear My voice,
and I know them, and they follow Me.
And I give them eternal life,
and they shall never perish;
neither shall anyone snatch them
out of My hand."

JOHN 10:27−28 NKJV

Thank You for the promise that I will hear Your voice, Lord. I know it is the sweetest sound my ears could ever distinguish.

Since I first heard Your call and responded to it, Your voice has directed my life. When I read Your Word, I hear it loudly and clearly, and Your Spirit speaks directly to my heart, showing me the way. Help me to follow closely on Your heels, my Shepherd.

Thank You for your promise that nothing will separate me from You and that I will spend eternity with You. I want to be with You forever.

On the Job

You must have accurate and
honest weights and measures,
so that you may live long in the land
the LORD your God is giving you.

DEUTERONOMY 25:15

With this verse, You're warning me that what I do in the workplace is as important to You as what I do in church, Lord. I have to admit that idea often makes me feel uncomfortable. Always doing right at work, as well as on my own time, can be a real challenge. It takes a total commitment to You, and sometimes that means standing up for or to others.

But I know that just as You promised the Israelites that You'd bless them, You will bless me, too. When I obey You, Your blessings loom large in my life. Help me remain faithful whether I'm on the job or in Your house, Lord.

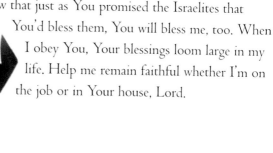

TRUSTWORTHINESS

*"Whoever can be trusted with very little
can also be trusted with much,
and whoever is dishonest with very little
will also be dishonest with much."*

LUKE 16:10

If I'm trustworthy, You'll trust me with many things, Lord. But if I can't be trusted with earthly goods, You'll not offer me many heavenly benefits. How much I have isn't the issue—where my heart is makes the difference, and I want my soul to be set firmly on You.

I can also apply this verse to other people. When others are trustworthy with small things, I'll be able to trust them with large ones. Help me understand people's souls by their actions. Let me recognize those who don't know You and pray for their hearts' redirection to faith.

Without You, Lord, none of us can be trusted for eternity.

GOD'S HONESTY

"And he who is the Glory of Israel will not lie,
nor will he change his mind,
for he is not human that
he should change his mind!"

1 SAMUEL 15:29 NLT

How glad I am, Lord, that I can trust You not to lie or change Your thinking. You follow through on every promise, and nothing ever alters Your perfection.

You want me to be honest, because that's what You are, and as I grow in You, I must increasingly reflect Your nature. Help me to become completely reliable. When I tell a friend I'll help out, I want him to be able to count on me. When a coworker needs the truth, let her be able to turn to me.

Every day, make me more like You, Lord. In my own strength, I'm only human, but Your Spirit makes me ever more like You.

TELLING THE TRUTH

No lie is of the truth.

1 JOHN 2:21 NASB

In our own power, we often try to combine truth and lies, Lord, to make a pleasing answer or get out of a difficult situation, but You promise that lies and truth cannot coexist. If I say something that's partly true, I'm still not telling the truth. If I hear something that contains a small lie, it still is not truth.

Cleanse my heart, Lord, and fill it with Your Spirit. I want Your truth to spill from my lips and be obvious in my every action. So fill me with such honesty that I will not displease You.

Help me discern truth in others, too. I do not want to trust in any lie.

IN CHRIST

At that time you were without Christ,
being aliens from the commonwealth of Israel
and strangers from the covenants of promise,
having no hope and without God in the world.
But now in Christ Jesus you who once were far off
have been brought near by the blood of Christ.

EPHESIANS 2:12–13 NKJV

Once I was far from You, Lord, and had no clear view of the future. I couldn't even have imagined a prospect that would gain me Your glorious heaven. Yet through Your sacrifice, Jesus, You drew me close to Yourself and gave me the hope of Your kingdom.

Without You, where would I be, Lord? My life would be desperately empty. I can't thank You enough for bringing Your love to me—but I want to show my appreciation by obeying You each day of my life.

HOPE IN TROUBLE

But the needy will not always be forgotten,
nor the hope of the afflicted ever perish.

PSALM 9:18

I certainly have needs now, Lord. They overwhelm me until I hardly know where to turn.

But I still hope in You, Jesus. I know You will never forget me or desert me, and You will always provide a way out of my troubles. No matter what problems we have faced, You have never yet forgotten or given up on Your people. Though it may take some time, You faithfully respond.

In my need, assuage my physical and spiritual emptiness, Lord. To have one need fulfilled without the other will not make me complete. Without Your Spirit's flow in my life, I am still afflicted. I need Your filling, Lord.

RENEWED STRENGTH

But those who hope in the LORD
will renew their strength.
They will soar on wings like eagles;
they will run and not grow weary,
they will walk and not be faint.

ISAIAH 40:31

What a soaring promise this is, Lord God, one all Your people treasure.

I've needed this promise, Lord, when work—for You or on the job—seemed too hard. I've wanted to soar, run, and walk for miles when my strength has been small and my heart has been heavy. You've empowered me to do that. Though the way may have been hard, You've given me energy to go on and prosper.

Your promise has already brought me strength in trials, but I know there's a lot more soaring to do. I want to finish my life in Your power and reach for eternity, too.

HOLY SPIRIT POWER

*And hope does not disappoint us,
because God has poured out his love
into our hearts by the Holy Spirit,
whom he has given us.
You see, at just the right time,
when we were still powerless,
Christ died for the ungodly.*

ROMANS 5:5–6

I've doubted, Lord, but You've never disappointed me. Though I've sometimes needed buckets of hope to get me through a day, Your love has always brought me through.

When I felt powerless in a situation, Your Spirit came alongside me and showed me the way. First, He drew me to accept Your sacrifice for me, Jesus. When I felt powerless, Your Spirit began to strengthen me to live for You.

Thank You for Your love and hope, Lord. I am not at all disappointed. Help me live in Your power today.

SHARING JESUS' SUFFERING

And since we are his children,
we will share his treasures—
for everything God gives to his Son,
Christ, is ours, too.
But if we are to share his glory,
we must also share his suffering.

ROMANS 8:17 NLT

How many blessings You've given me, Lord. But just because I'm blessed with Your love doesn't mean I miss out on the hard times.

I have to admit I like the idea of sharing Your treasures. That's the good part of this promise. I'm not so excited about sharing suffering. But help me to realize that these sufferings are shared. Whatever I have to go through, I don't do alone. Jesus, You've been there before me, and You walk by my side.

Thank You for sharing the hurts as well as the good things in life. I love You, Lord.

OVERCOMING DEATH

*"He who overcomes will not be hurt
at all by the second death."*

REVELATION 2:11

osing a loved one deeply hurts me, Lord. All humanity seems to have a spark of eternity, and when I lose someone, it just doesn't seem right. Somewhere deep inside, I know people weren't created simply to die.

Your Word proves that when it says death isn't the end. Whether or not they know You, humans have an eternal destination. When the one whose life ends exhales that last breath, eternity in heaven or hell begins. Those of us who believe are not harmed by death as we pass into eternity, but those who don't know You fall into eternal torment.

I don't want anyone I know to succumb to eternal death, so help me reach them with Your Word. May they never experience the pain of a Jesusless eternity.

OVERCOMING HARDSHIP

You have allowed me to suffer much hardship,
but you will restore me to life again and
lift me up from the depths of the earth.

PSALM 71:20 NLT

When life gets hard, Lord, I sometimes wish the hurt would end or that I could run away from it. Pressure doesn't feel good, and I simply want to escape. But even when I feel a lot of pain, remind me that none of it is out of Your control. Though I may not understand pain's purpose, You have allowed this into my life to create something good.

When I face hardship, help me through it—then restore me to life. Instead of leaving me in the valley, bring me up the mountainside so I can see Your plan anew.

COMFORT IN SUFFERING

You can be sure that the more we suffer for Christ,
the more God will shower us with
his comfort through Christ.

2 CORINTHIANS 1:5 NLT

I may not have suffered as much as some Christians, but I know the truth of this verse, Lord. When I've endured trials for You, I've felt the comfort of another Christian or the warmth of Your Spirit encouraging me. The worse the suffering has been, the greater the response You've provided for me.

Whatever I experience, whether I face a massive life change or the doorway to eternity, I can always trust that You will be there comforting me. I may not be able to get through this on my own, but with You, I can manage anything.

Thank You, Jesus, for Your merciful love.

BLESSINGS OF WORK

*For the LORD your God will bless you
in all your harvest and in
all the work of your hands,
and your joy will be complete.*

DEUTERONOMY 16:15

I'll admit I don't always recognize the blessings of work, Lord. When things are too challenging, it's hard to imagine any job is a blessing. When I have to find a new, permanent job that will help me plan my future, "blessing" may not be the first word that comes to mind.

But like the people who celebrated their harvest, I like knowing that my life is provided for. Having a regular paycheck shows You are caring for my life. So put me in the place where You'd have me work. As I labor for You, Lord, You bless me, and I discover the complete joy of relying on You.

PERSISTENCY

*"But you, be strong and
do not let your hands be weak,
for your work shall be rewarded!"*

2 CHRONICLES 15:7 NKJV

Lord, though You gave this promise to King Asa, I know it's also true for me. When I work hard, You can bless me in many ways.

Right now, as I seek work, help me do so consistently, as if I were working for You, not just myself. When I send out many resumes and get few responses, keep me going even when discouragement tempts me to quit.

If I keep my hands strong, typing at the computer or filling out applications for work, I know You will be faithful. Eventually I'll find the job You had in mind for me all along.

Justice

The LORD gives righteousness and justice
to all who are treated unfairly.

Psalm 103:6 NLT

S ometimes it just doesn't seem right, Lord. I apply for a job that seems perfect, but I never hear back. Or I go for an interview and can tell that the person I'm talking to will reject me for all the wrong reasons.

If I am treated unfairly, help me to trust in You, Lord. If that person rejects me wrongly, You can make it right. All I need to do is trust Your righteousness and believe You have something even better for me. Since You manage the entire universe, how can I imagine that You can't control this small problem?

I'm putting my faith in You, Lord—no matter how people treat me.

GOD'S FAITHFULNESS

He hath said,
I will never leave thee, nor forsake thee.

HEBREWS 13:5 KJV

ob hunting is tough, Lord. No matter what the economy is like, putting yourself on the line before a person you don't even know is hard. Finding the best answers to every question takes a lot of thought and quick response time.

I'm so glad that You are with me even in this. You don't stand outside the door during my interview; You're in that room with me. Even when I'm suffering doubt or disappointment in my job search, You're paving the way to my future.

Thank You for standing by me in every situation. When I get that new job, we'll have a real praise party together.

GOD'S COMING JUDGMENT

Then the trees of the forest will sing,
they will sing for joy before the LORD,
for he comes to judge the earth.

1 CHRONICLES 16:33

I don't often think about joy and Your judgment in the same moment, Lord. Too many people who don't know You make me think of things other than how wonderful Your return will be. Right now, I focus more on reaching out to those who have yet to come to You in faith.

But one day, the entire earth will rejoice as You take control of the world that has always been Yours. The time for accepting You will be past, and You will judge according to the choices we've already made. Then I will sing with the trees of the forest and the rest of the earth. How wonderful to see my Lord, in whom I've believed!

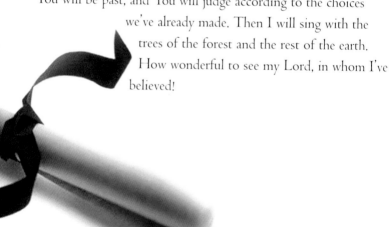

GOD'S STRENGTH

"The joy of the LORD is your strength."
NEHEMIAH 8:10 NKJV

I know I'm not much in my own power, Lord. Even at my strongest, life can turn me inside out in a moment, whether it's physically or spiritually. It doesn't take a lot to humble me.

But in You I can rejoice instead of worrying about my limitations. As I tap into Your power and authority, the challenges lessen. Instead of spending my time worrying about a problem, I can sing Your praises and share my faith in You. As my focus shifts from myself to You, Your joy fills my heart.

Thank You, Jesus, for being my strength. I rejoice in Your love and care for me.

LIVING WITH GOD

You will show me the way of life,
granting me the joy of your presence
and the pleasures of living with you forever.

PSALM 16:11 NLT

on-Christians just can't imagine the joy of living with You for eternity, Lord. I've seen it in a thousand ways as they reject You because You don't meet "their standards." It makes me sad to think of all the fun they're missing in life because of their mistaken ideas.

I'm so glad that living with You, both here on earth and in heaven, isn't the miserable matter they think it is. How can anyone who hasn't known You imagine the peace and joy knowing You brings?

Thank You for showing me the way of life. Help me to live out a testimony that leads others to joy in You, too.

SEEING JESUS

"Truly, you will weep and mourn over
what is going to happen to me,
but the world will rejoice.
You will grieve,
but your grief will suddenly turn to
wonderful joy when you see me again."

JOHN 16:20 NLT

How sorrowful Your death made Your disciples, Lord. Yet You promised a sudden flood of joy would overtake them when they saw You again.

I look forward to the same joy on the day when I see You, Jesus. Today, when the world pushes in on me and life feels miserable—even though I'm following You—that future becomes one of my greatest hopes. I want to see You soon and be as close to You as possible. Nothing on this earth could compare with sharing eternity with You.

Thank You for that upcoming joy, Lord. I can hardly wait.

GOD'S FRIENDSHIP

"For the LORD *your God,*
He is the One who goes with you.
He will not leave you nor forsake you."

DEUTERONOMY 31:6 NKJV

No matter whether I face a difficult situation physically, spiritually, or emotionally, I can relax, knowing You never give up on me, Lord. When others desert me because my life is a mess or they are afraid to get involved, You remain right by my side.

Thank You for Your continual faithfulness. When my heart feels empty because others have given up on me, Your Spirit offers comfort. Even when I don't feel You there, I can still trust You are right by my side. Though I can't always count on other people, You remain with me through both trials and blessings. There's no one I'd rather share both with.

GOD'S RESCUE

My eyes are continually toward the LORD,
for He will pluck my feet out of the net.
Turn to me and be gracious to me,
for I am lonely and afflicted.

PSALM 25:15−16 NASB

When I'm hurting, I'm glad others try to ease my pain. But often they provide only limited answers or solutions to my grief. No matter who else stands by me, when I'm lonely and aching, Lord, I need Your all-powerful healing touch. Only You can reach the agonizing places that no one else can get to. Though people do their best to give me good advice or comfort, only Your Spirit touches my innermost spots.

Others try to rescue me, but only You can take complete charge of the situation and bring relief. I need Your hand on my life when I feel lonely and afflicted. Thank You for Your aid, Lord.

FEELING FAR FROM GOD

*"But from there you will seek the LORD your God,
and you will find Him if you search for Him
with all your heart and all your soul."*

DEUTERONOMY 4:29 NASB

Sometimes when I hurt, I feel so far from You, Lord, that I begin to wonder if You even care anymore. When I experience that feeling, often it's because the world has gotten in between us. I've fallen into sin, and the sin looks good. Or I've let the pressures of overbusyness keep me from time with You. Forgive me, Lord.

A life off course becomes a lonely existence. Even in a crowd, I feel far from everyone. All I need to do is return to You. Turn my heart again in the right direction, Lord. Help me put aside all that divides us and draw close to Your side again.

FAMILY

God sets the lonely in families.

PSALM 68:6

Thank You for giving me a built-in loneliness remover, Lord. You've given me my family to let me know that I'm not unaccompanied in this world. I have people who care about me and to whom I can turn in an empty time.

Though I may not always agree with my parents or siblings, Lord, You've put me together with these people for life. Help me to develop the best relationship possible with each family member so we can share our lives in peace. We need to turn to each other when the rest of the world attacks and to find solace in each other, as well as in You. Bring comfort and strong relationships to our home.

UNFAILING LOVE

Love never fails.

1 CORINTHIANS 13:8 NKJV

I couldn't call my love for others "unfailing," Lord. When people irritate me, it's so easy to make unloving choices. Though I want to draw others to You by my own faithfulness, my own sin gets in the way, and I find myself being a traitor to Your kingdom.

Though my caring ability fails often, I know from experience and Your Word that Yours never does. I'm incredibly glad of this promise, because I know how much I need Your love every moment of my life. If You failed to shower me with Your affection, my days would really be a mess.

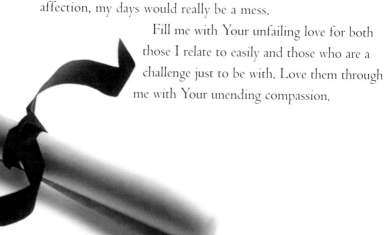

Fill me with Your unfailing love for both those I relate to easily and those who are a challenge just to be with. Love them through me with Your unending compassion.

FORGIVING LOVE

"Don't tear your clothing in your grief;
instead, tear your hearts."
Return to the LORD your God,
for he is gracious and merciful.
He is not easily angered.
He is filled with kindness and
is eager not to punish you.

JOEL 2:13 NLT

When I've done wrong, it's comforting to know You want me to return to You, Lord. Though it seems right that You should hold my sin against me, that's not Your desire. You've already forgiven my sin with Jesus' sacrifice. I need simply turn to You and acknowledge my unfaithfulness.

Turn my heart from wrongdoing, Lord. I don't want to miss out on a moment of Your love and grace. Draw me close, Jesus, to Your wounded side, where I can rejoice in Your forgiving love.

LOVE COVERS SINS

Hatred stirs up strife,
but love covers all sins.
PROVERBS 10:12 NKJV

ometimes it's easier to stir up strife than cover sins, Lord.
When another person wrongs me, it's often my first
response; I look to get even, not bring peace to our
relationship. But stirring things up is a sinful reaction, one that
denies Your love and spreads sin, both in my heart and in the
hearts of others.

I don't want to live that way, Jesus. But as hard as I try to
change things, I continually fail. Only Your Spirit can transform
me. Cover my sins with Your love and fill my spirit with the
desire to do Your will. As I learn to forgive, fill me with love
that reflects Yours so I can truly live for You.

GOD'S REDEEMING LOVE

[God] redeems your life from the pit
and crowns you with love and compassion.

Bound by sin, my life was worthy of a pit, Lord. But You came and redeemed me. The transformation Your love made in me can hardly be explained.

Thank You for buying me back from sin before I was even born. Two thousand years ago, when Your Son died on the cross for my sins, You made the transaction. But those years between have no influence as Your redemption powerfully impacts my life.

Not only have You saved me, Lord, You've crowned my life with love and compassion. As You have blessed my life so incredibly, help me use those blessings to reach out to all who need Your redeeming love.

DISHONEST GAIN

Wealth gained by dishonesty will be diminished,
but he who gathers by labor will increase.

PROVERBS 13:11 NKJV

It hurts when I see people who gain their money illicitly, Lord. Sometimes I feel so angry at the way they've cheated others for their own gain. But I know, however much it bothers me, it must bother You even more. Perhaps that's why You gave us this promise that people never really gain when they're greedy.

When I feel like pointing the finger at others, though, remind me of my own financial affairs and my need to be honest, too. Before I can accuse another, I must be certain that I'm following Your will. Turn my eyes to my own obedience, and let it be complete. Help me to work hard for all I get.

MONEY NEVER SATISFIES

He who loves silver will not be satisfied with silver;
nor he who loves abundance, with increase.
This also is vanity.

ECCLESIASTES 5:10 NKJV

I have to admit I'd like to have many things, Lord. Financial success and blessings could make life easier in some ways. But You're reminding me that seeking them as my final goal is useless. Money won't fill the ache in a heart, and a successful career won't solve every problem in life.

May my satisfaction never be with things, Lord. I don't want to come to the end of my life and find I have nothing to show for it. Remind me that money and property do not translate into heavenly rewards—those are found in a giving heart and love for You.

SERVING GOD

"No one can serve two masters.
Either he will hate the one and love the other,
or he will be devoted to the one
and despise the other.
You cannot serve both God and Money."

MATTHEW 6:24

Lord, You promise that I can't serve You and another master, especially when that master is money. Though people speak of "the almighty dollar," there's nothing almighty about it—nor about pounds, pesos, francs, or any other currency.

Only You are truly almighty. Serving You brings any believer a power that money can never offer—the power to store up valuables for eternity, not simply for a few years on earth. Keep me mindful of that truth, Lord. May my eyes always be on You, not on my pocketbook or bank account.

THE VALUE OF KNOWLEDGE

Gold there is, and rubies in abundance,
but lips that speak knowledge are a rare jewel.

PROVERBS 20:15

Lord, You know gold and jewels have their attraction for me. The things of this world look good to me, or they'd never be a temptation. Satan is aware of that and uses things to his advantage. But You've warned me that the real jewels of heaven do not sparkle physically. Knowledge of You and Your Word are the truly valuable things—on earth and in heaven.

I may never own the jewels and metals many people treasure here, but I'm glad I know You and can send this jewel into eternity. Earning Your "well done" means more to me than any earthly thing.

Tongue Follows Heart

Before a word is on my tongue
you know it completely, O Lord.

PSALM 139:4

I can't keep a secret from You, Lord, because every word I speak is part of an open book. Before a syllable falls off my tongue, You know my thoughts and emotions. Words can't consistently hide feelings; eventually they'll directly reflect my heart and soul. In a sentence that shows what I really feel, truth finally comes out.

When I follow You closely, I need not worry. My words glorify You. Yet when I stray from You, my language changes, and people observe the alteration in my heart. Only if my heart is Yours will my words be, too, Lord. May both constantly focus on You.

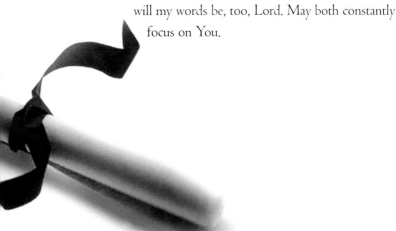

Rescued!

The words of the wicked lie in wait for blood,
but the speech of the upright rescues them.

PROVERBS 12:6

I never thought of my words rescuing me, Lord. But I can see that good words keep me from harm and even protect me when it threatens. Under my own power I cannot utter only rescuing words, but when Your Spirit guides my speech, it's wiser and kinder. Without Your direction in my life, I would say things that hurt and harm.

When I hear the wicked speech of others, don't let me fall into their patterns. Turn my ears away from sin to hear Your still, small voice instead. I need Your Word to guide my heart and mouth so that my words will help instead of shed blood.

A Soul Snare

A fool's mouth is his destruction,
and his lips are the snare of his soul.

Proverbs 18:7 KJV

In Your Word, Lord, You describe a fool as someone who does not know You. As I've watched those who know You and those who don't, I see that Christians may not always say the right words and give a perfect testimony—but how their speech differs from those with no regard for You. The heart change You give affects the mouth because it alters the soul.

When others' voices show no respect for You, Lord, I can discern the speakers' hearts. Instead of getting myself lost in anger at their speech, help me pray for the souls they reflect. May Your wisdom direct me to plant a seed that may bring them to You.

KEEPING PROMISES

[He] who keeps his oath even when it hurts. . .
will never be shaken.

PSALM 15:4−5

I've made promises, Almighty Lord, and not kept them—because it wasn't convenient or I discovered they were unwise. I've let people down when I should have been faithful. Forgive me for not standing firm and reflecting Your trustworthy character. I'm thankful You don't treat promises as lightly as I do.

You pledge that, when I keep my promises, You will not let me be shaken. Though I may think I've made a mistake, You can still make it right if I'm faithful to my word.

Before I pledge to do something, help me to think carefully and seek Your wisdom, Lord. Once I tell someone to count on me, I want to follow through. After all, I've seen Your example, Jesus. You've kept every promise You've given me.

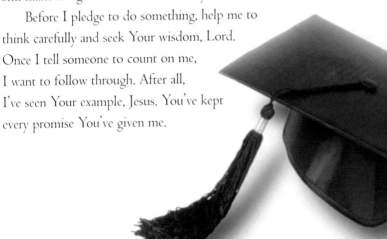

ALL THINGS NEW

And he that sat upon the throne said,
Behold, I make all things new.

REVELATION 21:5 KJV

You have made all things new for me, Lord. You promise a new heaven and earth at the end of time, but only those whose lives are already changed will live there. Thank You for making me a completely different person with a heart that's Yours for eternity.

When I look at my life, I see newness in my thoughts, words, and actions. There's no corner of my life You haven't changed or don't desire to impact. Spread Your fresh life to every corner of my being—heart, soul, and mind.

As I walk in Your life I turn away from old sin. Keep me from that worn-out place and fresh in Your Spirit.

RAISED TO NEW LIFE

We were therefore buried with him
through baptism into death in order that,
just as Christ was raised from the dead
through the glory of the Father,
we too may live a new life.

ROMANS 6:4

Such an amazing idea is hard to take in, Lord. Through baptism, which identifies me with You, I am raised up, just as You raised Your Son, Jesus, from the dead. My sins remain behind, and my life is new.

Help me to live this new life to glorify You, keeping ever before my face the truth that sin is behind me. I don't want to remain in the old place when You've gifted me with so much that's fresh—and infinitely better.

Keep me faithful in Your new life, Lord. Each day may I walk beside You.

A NEW PERSON

What this means is that those who
become Christians become new persons.
They are not the same anymore,
for the old life is gone.
A new life has begun!

2 CORINTHIANS 5:17 NLT

I know this promise is true, Lord, because I've felt it in my own life. The person I used to be is gone, and You've put a new life in my heart and soul. Things I could never have imagined believing have become real to me as I've immersed myself in Your Word.

When I feel tempted to fall back into my old ways, remind me how You've worked in my soul and mind. Thank You for this new life. I don't want to waste a moment of it. Help me to become exactly the person You want me to be—one who glorifies You in every action and thought.

FINDING LIFE

"Whoever finds his life will lose it,
and whoever loses his life
for my sake will find it."

MATTHEW 10:39

The new life You promise, Lord, isn't simply for a few years—not even one hundred of them. Your life lasts forever, and I will share eternity with You. That's why You tell me not to cling too closely to this world. Eternity doesn't depend on my going with the crowd here on earth, because their choices don't last. It doesn't require that I please anyone but You.

I want to use this life to make a difference for eternity. In the here and now I can share Your love with those who don't yet know You and those who struggle to live their new lives well. Whatever I lose in this world, let it be for gain in Your kingdom.

FAITH TESTED

*The testing of your faith
produces patience.*
JAMES 1:3 NKJV

I don't enjoy having my faith tested, Lord. It can hurt deeply, and I'd avoid many such challenges if I could. But You, knowing what's best for me, don't let me get away with that attitude. Instead, You toss me into situations I don't like because they'll make me stronger. As situations or people irritate me and I stand firm, I become more patient.

I'd never think of asking for trials, but without them I'd never be longsuffering with others. I'd never gain Your character, and I wouldn't put up with much.

Thank You for the trials I try to avoid. They've been a blessing to me.

A PATIENT SPIRIT

The end of a thing is better than its beginning;
the patient in spirit is better than the proud in spirit.

ECCLESIASTES 7:8 NKJV

I've been proud, Lord, so I understand what You're talking about here. At times that old haughty spirit still tempts me. I want things my way, and I don't want to wait for Your better path.

But You didn't leave me to my own desires. You're working in me, slowly but surely, to turn that pride into forbearance. You're strengthening my "patience muscles" as I grow in faith.

In the end, I will be better than I was on the first day I came to You. The proud spirit that once indwelled me has turned soft and gentle—but strong. I'd never have done that under my own power. Thank You for Your Spirit's work in my heart.

THE POWER OF PATIENCE

Through patience a ruler can be persuaded,
and a gentle tongue can break a bone.

PROVERBS 25:15

Too often, to me, success means getting an immediate "yes" from my boss or other leader. I want an answer now, and I want it to be positive.

But You're promising me, Lord, that persuasion can be powerful if I don't give up too quickly. Such gentle but firm tactics can be Your will when direct, insistent ones would fail.

Give me Your wisdom so I know when to be patient and persistent about changing another's mind. Though soft words may not seem powerful, You're telling me they are, Lord—and I need to take Your advice.

SUFFER PATIENTLY

But when you do good and suffer,
if you take it patiently,
this is commendable before God.

1 PETER 2:20 NKJV

When I'm suffering, I really need patience, Lord. Putting up with something uncomfortable isn't easy, and I'm tempted to become angry or cranky when things don't go my way. Your peace and patience help me deal with problems I can't handle on my own.

Others may not appreciate my hurts, Lord. They'll try to tell me I did something wrong even when I know I've done my best to obey You. I need Your Spirit to be patient with them and trust that even if no human understands my situation, You do.

Keep me faithful in suffering, to earn Your approval—not that of others. Thank You for loving me, Lord, even when I hurt.

PEACEFUL HARVEST

And those who are peacemakers
will plant seeds of peace and
reap a harvest of goodness.

JAMES 3:18 NLT

Lord, when I try to make peace with others in my world,
I often think of the blessings of not having arguments,
problems, and unresolved issues. I can't say I really look
at the big picture, when just having the immediate blessing seems
so good. But You promise me that as I make peace with
friends, family, and coworkers, I will reap something
else—goodness.

I'm thankful that Your blessings
are not small ones. As I obey
You for the little things, You often give
me an extra, even better blessing. Thank
You for Your generosity. With this second
harvest I want to do good for others, as
well as myself.

Peace of Mind

"I am leaving you with a gift—
peace of mind and heart.
And the peace I give isn't like
the peace the world gives.
So don't be troubled or afraid."

John 14:27 NLT

You know fear comes easily in this world, Lord. Maybe it's because You recognized how much we need Your special peace—surpassing anything this world has to offer—that You left Your people with this promise. Real peace is hard to come by here on earth.

When troubles come, help me to rest in You, Jesus, instead of accepting the world's turmoil. Truly, Your harmony isn't anything like this world's attempts at peacemaking—it reaches to my heart and soul and changes my life entirely. With it, the distress of the world remains at bay.

Thank You, Lord, for Your peace.

A HEALTHFUL PEACE

A heart at peace gives life to the body,
but envy rots the bones.

PROVERBS 14:30

Your peace not only affects my soul, Lord, it also brings life to my body. If I no longer encourage harmful emotions that increase the wear and tear on my frame, and if my spirit is resting in You, every part of my anatomy benefits.

When I'm tempted to feel envy, lust, and other harmful emotions, remind me of this promise and help me to put all evil aside. Cleanse my heart, Lord, and enable me to live instead in Your Spirit. Let me be at peace with You, Jesus. I want to be completely at rest and healthy in body, mind, and soul.

PEACE WITH ENEMIES

When a man's ways are pleasing to the LORD,
he makes even his enemies live at peace with him.

PROVERBS 16:7

I want to please You because I love You, Lord. But it's wonderful to recognize that as I obey You, You give me more than peace with Yourself—You also offer me peace with others, even those who don't agree with me. When I live a right life, You bless my whole being with contentment.

I want to live at peace with others, Lord, even those who don't like me or who hate my faith. But even more, I want them to know You, too. Bring them peace in their hearts, and we will be completely at peace in You.

ANSWERED PRAYER

"And whatever things you ask in prayer,
believing, you will receive."

MATTHEW 21:22 NKJV

What a tremendous promise this is, Lord. As You open heaven's treasures to me in these few words, I see exactly how much You love me.

I know I can't take advantage of Your love, Lord. Like a good earthly father, You never allow me to have anything that would really harm me, no matter how much I demand it. But as my faith grows, I begin to ask for things that benefit Your kingdom, instead of fulfilling my greed. The more I know You, the more I pray in Your will, and the more You answer with a "yes."

Help me to ask for the right things, Lord, and give me faith to believe You'll provide them. Then when I receive my answer, we'll both be blessed.

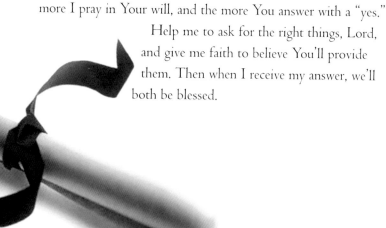

PERSISTENT PRAYER

"Ask, and it will be given to you;
seek, and you will find;
knock, and it will be opened to you.
For everyone who asks receives,
and he who seeks finds,
and to him who knocks it will be opened."

MATTHEW 7:7−8 NKJV

I've asked for things in prayer and not gotten them, Lord. Then I've started to wonder if I should have asked at all. But this verse encourages me not only to ask once, but to seek and knock persistently for the good things of Your kingdom.

When I don't get an immediate answer, Lord, remind me to check with You to make sure my request is good—and then to keep on trusting and persisting. Even if I don't get the response I want, I know you don't ignore my prayers. You will answer when the time is right.

Thank You, Lord, for Your answers to every prayer.

RIGHTEOUS PRAYER

*Confess your sins to each other and
pray for each other so that you may be healed.
The earnest prayer of a righteous person
has great power and wonderful results.*

JAMES 5:16 NLT

Though I may feel like going it on my own, Lord, You're telling me to join with other Christians in prayer—especially with those who closely follow Your will. When my own prayers seem to simply hit the ceiling, I can benefit from another faithful Christian's perspective and steadfastness.

Whether I need healing of the heart or body, help me to turn to others, confess whatever sins I've committed and not brought to You, and ask for Your mending. When strong believers pray for me, I feel Your power and its wonderful results.

GOD HEARS PRAYER

The LORD is far from the wicked
but he hears the prayer of the righteous.

PROVERBS 15:29

A mazing, Lord—You hear every request I pray! Even when I don't receive a quick response or when You say "no," You have listened to my supplication. As I ask for the wrong things, You hear that prayer, see to its heart, and work out my problem in a better way that accomplishes Your will. Though I haven't perfectly understood Your ways, You're always open to me.

Because I've accepted Jesus, You've called me righteous and listen to me. But those who don't love Your Son are far from Your ears. They cannot count on answered prayer until they turn to You. Bring them to faith in You, Lord, so You can hear their supplications, too.

RESPECT FOR OTHERS

"Watch out!
Be on your guard against all kinds of greed;
a man's life does not consist in the
abundance of his possessions."

LUKE 12:15

Though the world values me according to what I own or how much I make in a year, I'm glad You don't, Lord. There is so much more to life than money and things. But I've noticed that even though I like being judged by better means, I often give a wealthy person more respect than the poor but faithful person.

Forgive me, Lord, for judging wrongly in such an important matter.

I want to value people as You do— so help me to view them through Your lens, not the world's. When I do that, I will befriend those who are important to You, even if they don't have a dime in their pockets.

GIFT OF GOD

As for every man to whom
God has given riches and wealth,
and given him power to eat of it,
to receive his heritage and rejoice in his labor—
this is the gift of God.

ECCLESIASTES 5:19 NKJV

Receiving gifts from You, whether spiritual or physical ones, is a blessing, Lord. But it's easy to forget that a paycheck, a new car, a great job, or a place to live come from Your hand as much as a spiritual endowment.

Thank You for every blessing, Lord. Help me to appreciate all You've given me and to thank You that You haven't presented me with inappropriate things I might misuse. You know the gifts I really need and the ones that would be bad for me.

When I receive Your favor, help me to share what I can generously. I want to reflect Your compassion and love.

OBEDIENCE AND BLESSINGS

"If you keep the commandments of
the LORD your God and walk in His ways. . .
the LORD will grant you plenty of goods,
in the fruit of your body,
in the increase of your livestock,
and in the produce of your ground,
in the land of which the LORD
swore to your fathers to give you."

DEUTERONOMY 28:9, 11 NKJV

O bedience has its blessings, Lord. Though I can't give my heart to You only for those blessings, Lord, when I honestly seek to obey You, You may overwhelm me with Your generosity.

You've already given me so much to be thankful for, Jesus. I thank You for family, work, and food on my table. No matter how much I have, as long as I have been faithful, You have always presented me with everything I need.

Keep me obedient to You today, Lord.

GENEROSITY

A generous man will prosper;
he who refreshes others will himself be refreshed.

PROVERBS 11:25

I want to be generous, Lord, because that's what You are. From the moment I accepted Your Son, I took part in Your spiritual blessings, experiencing freedom from sin. But You've also given me physical and intellectual blessings I can share with others. I cannot rightly withhold anything You ask me to use to help another.

As I give to others, You promise to refresh me. Sometimes You revive me spiritually instead of returning a physical blessing, but You always give generously, beyond what I expected.

Thank You for giving me so much, Lord. Help me not to hoard, but to share Your prosperity.

BLESSED BY GOD

He who has clean hands and a pure heart,
who has not lifted up his soul to falsehood
and has not sworn deceitfully.
He shall receive a blessing from the LORD
and righteousness from the God of his salvation.

PSALM 24:4–5 NASB

This is a tall order, Lord. Who among us has never perpetrated a falsehood on another or lied when confronted with wrongdoing? But that's not the lifestyle You want us to lead, and in Your Spirit, we can have the clean hands and pure heart You require of us.

Cleanse me and fill me with Your Spirit, Lord. Make me entirely clean in You through Your salvation. Then build in me a life that reflects that change. As I put every part of my being in Your hands, I am blessed beyond measure.

Thank You, Lord, for Your new life in my life.

GOD'S GOODNESS

Truly God is good to Israel,
to such as are pure in heart.

PSALM 73:1 NKJV

Heart purity only comes from You, Lord. On our own, none of us could attain Your righteousness. Our sins—even the petty ones—separate us entirely from You.

Thank You for coming into my heart, Jesus, and giving me the squeaky cleanness only You offer. Yet that's only the way You began Your blessings. Each day You consistently help me live pure-heartedly and reflect Your goodness and love. I could never repay You for all You've done in my soul.

May my life become a vivid testimony to others who search for goodness. I want You to bless them as much as You've blessed me—to let them join Your faithful ones. Then together we will praise You, our good God, throughout eternity.

HEART PURITY

"Blessed are the pure in heart,
for they will see God."

MATTHEW 5:8

When purity of heart, mind, and soul seems difficult, remind me of this promise, Lord. Seeing You is the greatest blessing I could receive—I especially long to look directly into Your face.

In this world, I cannot see You fully, though every day I perceive more of Your love, grace, and blessing as I draw nearer to You in obedience. I cannot see You physically, yet I get a clearer spiritual picture of You every day as I live out Your commands. Reading Your Word, praying, and acting in a way that pleases You make You ever clearer to my heart and soul.

Make my heart increasingly pure, Lord. Long before we meet face-to-face I want to know You well.

LIFE PURITY

Wives, in the same way be
submissive to your husbands so that,
if any of them do not believe the word,
they may be won over without words
by the behavior of their wives,
when they see the purity
and reverence of your lives.

1 PETER 3:1–2

Just imagine—I can live so well in purity that I win someone to You, Lord! What a blessing to know that a spotless life that depicts Your love can bring those I love to faith, even if I don't say a word.

Thank You, Jesus, for making my life that valuable. Help me to live so well that I become a beacon to my family and friends. Every day I want to shine forth Your love and grace.

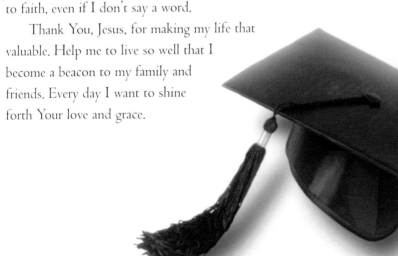

DELIVERANCE FROM TROUBLES

A righteous man may have many troubles,
but the LORD delivers him from them all.

PSALM 34:19

Thank You for reminding me that troubles don't mean You have forgotten me, Lord. Problems in my life don't show that You've given up on me or that I am not obeying You. I'm so glad that You have promised to help me through every trouble I ever face.

On my own, I could never handle every challenge that came along—but knowing You will be with me through thick and thin raises my spirits. No problem is too large for You. You'll see me through no matter how many dilemmas lie before me.

Thank You, Lord, for Your deliverance from difficulties large and small. I need Your help for each, and I'm blessed to have such a caring Father.

REWARDS FOR RIGHTEOUSNESS

*"The LORD rewards every man for
his righteousness and faithfulness."*

1 SAMUEL 26:23

When it seems hard to do Your will and remain faithful to You, Lord, I need to keep this promise in mind. Trials seem much lighter when I focus on the truth that Your rewards will follow.

Help me daily to live a righteous, faithful life in You instead of becoming distracted by the world's toys. The rewards offered by sin are few and short-term compared to Yours. Though they attract for a little while, they cannot bless me forever.

Thank You, Jesus, for Your many blessings in this life and the hereafter. Today I want to live for Your eternal rewards. Show me how I can do that with each moment of my time.

GOD LOVES RIGHTEOUSNESS

He [God] loves righteousness and justice;
the earth is full of the goodness of the LORD.

PSALM 33:5 NKJV

The whole world should be aware of Your goodness, Lord. You've filled the earth with it, from the amazing detail with which You've created our planet to the wonderful personal experiences You offer us. But somehow, we often still miss that truth. Those who don't know You can't understand the way Your righteousness and justice work in our fallen world. Even when believers face troubles, we can begin to doubt.

When I don't see Your hand through the world's injustice and wrongdoing, clearly show me Your truth so I can rejoice in this promise. As I trust that Your goodness is faithful, I can show others the way to You, too.

LIVING BY FAITH

"Behold the proud,
his soul is not upright in him;
but the just shall live by his faith."
HABAKKUK 2:4 NKJV

Lord, the idea of being upright, standing tall for You in faith and following Your ways, isn't very popular today. But when the world doesn't approve of my faith in You, please remind me that this isn't a popularity contest. Whether or not people agree with me doesn't matter as long as I'm doing what You ask me to do.

In eternity, how much I agreed with my friends or family won't matter so much. But how well I lived out my belief in You will pave the way for my place in Your kingdom. When I think of it that way, there should be no contest for my heart. Make me faithful to You.

GREATNESS IN SERVICE

"The greatest among you
will be your servant."

MATTHEW 23:11

I t's hard to think of greatness in servanthood, Lord. Our world doesn't think that way, and breaking out of the mold takes effort. Even in church I can have a hard time seeing greatness as a matter of doing things for others.

Help me change my thinking, Jesus, and help me model the lifestyle You want every Christian to have. Instead of seeking personal fame or self-importance, I need to help others and aid them in drawing closer to You. When other people see my actions, I want them to see You.

Help me become Your servant in every way, Lord. Then I'll have the only greatness worth having—I will be distinguished in Your eyes.

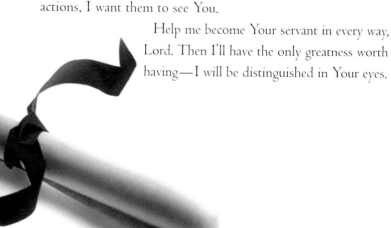

WHOLEHEARTED SERVICE

"No servant can serve two masters;
for either he will hate the one and love the other,
or else he will be devoted to
one and despise the other.
You cannot serve God and wealth."

LUKE 16:13 NASB

Many desirable things quickly turn me from You, Lord. I admit I willingly fall far from You when worldly toys attract me. Forgive me for placing anything ahead of Your love.

Though deep down I know things can never replace You, when money or goods attract me, I don't usually ponder the exchange I'd be making. I want to believe I can have it all. Remind me, Lord, that to be faithful to You, even my money must serve You. Spiritual things have so much more value than the wealth I desire.

Make me wholeheartedly desire Your will, Jesus, so I cannot serve the wrong master.

FOLLOWING JESUS

"Whoever serves me must follow me;
and where I am, my servant also will be.
My Father will honor the one who serves me."

JOHN 12:26

Jesus, I want to be where You are, not miles away trying to fulfill my own needs. Instead of seeking my own path, I must listen to Your call on my life and put Your commands into action. I must hear Your Word each day and listen to Your still, small voice as it speaks to my heart.

If I follow closely, You promise that Your Father will honor me. Though that honor can't be my only reason for obeying You, I'm thankful for the rewards my obedience will earn. I need the blessings You offer, Lord.

END OF THE CURSE

No longer will anything be cursed.
For the throne of God and
of the Lamb will be there,
and his servants will worship him.

REVELATION 22:3 NLT

What a glorious time this will be, Lord, when sin no longer rules the world. In Your eternal kingdom, all those who believe will do nothing but worship You. Satan will no longer trap us, and our minds and spirits will totally focus on You.

I can't quite imagine what heaven will be like, Lord, but I look forward to a time without sin, when I can draw close to You in a new way and serve You perfectly. When life becomes hard, I focus on this promise. I long to be with You for eternity, Jesus.

Thank You for this eternal promise.

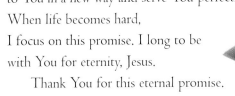

SIN FORGIVEN

"Blessed is the man whose sin
the Lord will never count against him."

ROMANS 4:8

Before I knew You, Lord, I could not understand the blessings of forgiven sin. But Your Spirit's cleansing and the freedom that followed faith are more wonderful than I ever could have imagined. Nothing the world offers can take their place.

Thank You for not counting my sin against me, but instead sending Your Son to take my place on the cross. If You'd left me to pay the price for my own wrongs, new life would have been impossible. But because You've put my sin away from me, everything's changed. Your pardon affects every corner of my being.

I'm totally blessed by Your forgiveness, Lord. Thank You from the bottom of my soul.

FREED FROM SIN

For sin shall not be master over you,
for you are not under law but under grace.

ROMANS 6:14 NASB

S in need not control me, Lord. You've promised that because of Your grace, no wrong thought or deed must rule me. Though I cannot keep each law perfectly, sin no longer controls my life. In Your eyes I am whole and pure because Your Son took my sin to the cross.

Thank You, Jesus, for dying in my place. Because of Your sacrifice, I experience Your powerful, life-changing grace. I'm glad You turned my heart to Yourself and saved my soul.

Fill me with Your Spirit, Lord, so I may live out Your grace today. I want to obey all Your commands. In You I'm free to do what's right, because sin no longer rules my heart.

God's Protection

We know that those who
have become part of God's family
do not make a practice of sinning,
for God's Son holds them securely,
and the evil one cannot get his hands on them.

1 John 5:18 nlt

I'm not perfect, Lord. You know the temptations I give in to each day. But as I've walked faithfully in You, You've made a great change in my life. Though I can't promise I'll never sin, You've cleansed my heart and soul and called me holy because of Your Son's sacrifice. Each day sin's hold on me lessens as I cling to You for help.

I couldn't avoid sin on my own. Thank You for holding tightly to me, keeping Satan far from me, and making me Yours for eternity. I want to draw closer to You each moment, Lord.

FORGIVING SIN

"For if you forgive men when they sin against you,
your heavenly Father will also forgive you."

MATTHEW 6:14

I t's chilling to think that I'll only be forgiven by You, Lord, as much as I forgive others. I have to admit that I'm hardly good at giving up my "right" to retribution when someone does me a serious wrong. Though I like to think I'm a good Christian, it's all too easy to want to get even.

Help me, Lord, to appreciate the forgiveness You've already given me—a forgiveness I didn't deserve. Then help me pass that attitude on to one who has hurt me deeply, so we'll both be free in You.

Thank You, Jesus, for the mercy I need each day, which You so readily provide. Let me give it freely wherever it's needed.

GOD'S PLAN

Commit to the LORD whatever you do,
and your plans will succeed.

PROVERBS 16:3

B y this promise, You've reminded me that I can never go it
alone—whatever I'm thinking of doing. From the
smallest thought to the most life-changing plan I'm
developing, I need Your input, advice, and direction.

If I don't follow You, I can end up in a terrible mess; but when
I commit my plans to You and act in a way that glorifies You, I
have prosperity. You will bring me through any challenge—at work,
at home, or in the spiritual realm. Though I may not ride on the
fast track to success, I will be on Your track to it, and that's what
ultimately matters to me.

If I have to choose between the world's
success and Yours, I'll go with Yours every
time, Lord.

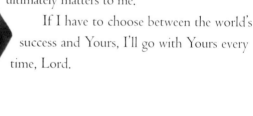

SUCCESS WITH GOD

There is no wisdom, no insight,
no plan that can succeed against the LORD.

PROVERBS 21:30

Success doesn't happen when a human tries to go against You, Lord. As I look at the methods people use to get ahead, I rejoice that You've given me this promise. I know that anything that ignores or defies Your wisdom will eventually fail.

I don't want to be one of those failures, Jesus. I'd rather follow Your wisdom, Your insight, and Your eternal plan. Keep me in Your way, no matter what "success method" others tout. If it doesn't glorify You, I want it to have no part in my life.

I need Your strength to keep my heart faithful, Jesus. Without You, I'm lost. Thank You for giving me Your power to succeed Your way.

Humility's Success

*The reward of humility and
the fear of the* Lord *are riches,
honor and life.*

Proverbs 22:4 nasb

What a promise You give me here, Lord. Though I tend to think non-Christians are the only ones who get ahead, You're telling me that that isn't true.

But humility doesn't come easily to me. So often I want to show my own greatness to the world instead of illustrating the greatness of Your humble Son. Jesus' humility gave me a place in heaven, yet I find it hard to walk in His footsteps.

Make me ever more faithful to You, Lord. I want to honor You and do all You command. Then You can give me whatever riches and honor You judge best, along with the new life You've promised me both here and in heaven.

GIVING

Honor the LORD from your wealth
and from the first of all your produce;
so your barns will be filled with plenty and
your vats will overflow with new wine.

PROVERBS 3:9–10 NASB

Giving seems like a funny way to be prosperous, Lord. It doesn't make sense that getting rid of wealth would bring anyone more abundance. But in Your kingdom, I've often seen Your plan work. I give to a cause You put on my heart, even though I don't have much to spare, and I never miss what I've given. Instead, You provide generously for my own needs.

Thank You, Lord, for blessing me so much. Help me give to bless others in turn. I don't want to hoard anything You've bestowed on me.

GOD CARES

Behold, the LORD's hand is not shortened,
that it cannot save; nor His ear heavy,
that it cannot hear.

ISAIAH 59:1 NKJV

I t warms my heart to know that You are not ignoring me even when I can't feel Your touch, Lord. If troubles face me and I'm tempted to think You don't care, You've promised me that that isn't so. You're still working in my life even if I can't sense it.

When You don't rush to my aid, You ask me to continue trusting in You. It's not time to give up. Though help isn't here yet, I can count on its being on the way.

I'm glad You hear my prayers and save me. If I have faith, Your hand will reach out to me at just the right moment. Thank You, Jesus, that Your salvation may be only a moment away.

GOD'S JUSTICE

It is only just for God to repay with
affliction those who afflict you,
and to give relief to you who are afflicted
and to us as well when the Lord Jesus will be revealed
from heaven with His mighty angels in flaming fire.

2 THESSALONIANS 1:6–7 NASB

When others cause me trouble, I may want to rush to gain revenge, but I don't have to. You, Lord, claim the privilege to bring justice to every hurt inflicted in the world. So when someone causes me pain, I can leave it in Your hands and know that in the end You will make things right.

Thank You for taking that burden from me, Jesus. No longer must I worry that someone will get away with wrongdoing. I need not sin while trying to make things "right." I'm glad I can trust in You to correct all wrongs.

SUFFERING

*"Do not fear any of those things
which you are about to suffer.
Indeed, the devil is about to throw
some of you into prison,
that you may be tested,
and you will have tribulation ten days.
Be faithful until death,
and I will give you the crown of life."*

REVELATION 2:10 NKJV

Not fearing suffering seems impossible, Lord. Suffering is not something any Christian looks forward to, yet all of us experience it in some way. Still, I know You have brought faithful believers through much more than I've experienced.

I haven't been imprisoned for my faith, Lord, but You promise You'll be there even if that should happen. Then if I stay faithful for a short time, I'll receive Your eternal crown of life and rejoice with You in heaven.

No matter what I suffer, keep me faithful to You, Jesus. I don't want anything to harm our relationship.

END OF SIN

Therefore, since Christ suffered for us in the flesh,
arm yourselves also with the same mind,
for he who has suffered in the flesh
has ceased from sin.

1 PETER 4:1 NKJV

Though I don't relish the tough times, Lord, I have to admit I'd like to be done with sin. No matter how much I try to avoid it, sin influences me constantly—and if I'm not careful, I easily find myself slipping into it again.

I'm glad my suffering has a purpose in Your plan, though I may not completely understand the details. How wonderful to know that suffering, however painful, will make me pure because of Your Son's sacrifice.

I want to cease from sin, Lord. Make me pure in You.

PERFECT PEACE

"You will keep him in perfect peace,
whose mind is stayed on You,
because he trusts in You."

ISAIAH 26:3 NKJV

Perfect peace—it's such a rarity in our world, Lord, where war and terrorism are common and confusion reigns. Left to ourselves, we'd never find real peace—the things we try to replace You with can never bring it to us.

But Your gracious love offers not simply peace for a time, but perfect peace. Minds focused on You cannot be disturbed, because human devices cannot destroy the trust that comes from a relationship with You.

I desperately need Your perfect peace, Jesus. Life tends to get in the way and turn me upside down. But You've promised this solution. Let me trust its truth and keep my mind stayed on You and You alone.

FAITHFUL GOD

And those who know Your name
will put their trust in You;
for You, LORD,
have not forsaken those who seek You.

Anyone who knows Your name—Your character—will trust in You, Jesus. What more could You sacrifice for us than Your life? And that gift of salvation was designed to benefit us.

When I think about Your faithfulness to Your people, I can't fathom it. So often we swerve in our belief. Distractions and temptations pull us far from You. Yet You have not given up on us, even when we would give up on ourselves. I know You've kept me seeking even when Your way seemed difficult to find.

Thank You for Your continued love and trust, Lord. Keep me doing Your will all my days.

REDEEMED BY GOD

The LORD redeems the soul of His servants,
and none of those who trust in Him
shall be condemned.

PSALM 34:22 NKJV

Y ou bought me out of sin, Lord, though I still struggle to make that truth complete in my life. I may attempt to completely understand this change, but it's beyond my finite mind. I recognize that You did not purchase only a portion of my life, but the whole thing—and every day You make me more like You. Thank You for giving me Your redemption in place of Satan's condemnation.

Help me to trust in You whenever I fall into sin. I need to know You care and still want to make me whole. Let my heart become tender to Your touch, and may I quickly confess all wrong. Then I can experience the peace You offer my soul.

GOD'S SALVATION

"My righteousness is near,
My salvation has gone forth,
and My arms will judge the peoples. . .
and on My arm they will trust. . . .
The heavens will vanish away like smoke,
the earth will grow old like a garment. . .
but My salvation will be forever,
and My righteousness will not be abolished."

ISAIAH 51:5–6 NKJV

One day this world will end, Lord. All I know will be gone, vanished like smoke. But even that will not be the end. It will only be the beginning of my time in eternity.

Though every physical thing vanishes, You've promised I can still trust in Your rescue— because Your salvation isn't for a moment in time, but forever.

Though all about me changes, You don't. Nothing can change Your covenant to save Your people.

Thank You for Your faithfulness, Lord, for all ages. I trust in You alone.

WISDOM WITH KNOWLEDGE

It is not good to have zeal
without knowledge,
nor to be hasty and miss the way.

PROVERBS 19:2

Lord, sometimes I rush into things without considering if I'm being wise—and that quick desire doesn't lead me in the right way. Forgive me for acting without thought and the prayer that would lead me in Your path.

I want to do right, to glorify You in all I think, do, and say. Usually, my desire to rush in is without deliberate disobedience. But without Your knowledge, I never end up in the right place. So keep me from quick but wrong reactions, and lead me by Your Spirit in Your way of wisdom.

ate Board of Education

Diploma

his certifies that
the bearer

pleted a Course of Study prescribed
Education and is entitled to this

Diploma

A NATION'S WISDOM

"You must obey these laws and regulations
when you arrive in the land you are
about to enter and occupy. . . .
If you obey them carefully,
you will display your wisdom and
intelligence to the surrounding nations.
When they hear about these laws, they will exclaim,
'What other nation is as wise and prudent as this!'"

DEUTERONOMY 4:5−6 NLT

Lord, You promise that Your laws and regulations that benefit me personally can also bless my country. It doesn't make me glad when our nation avoids Your truth to follow human plans.

When I have the chance to vote, Lord, help me to cast my ballot for those who also glorify You and follow Your laws. Please give me people to vote for who love You and want our nation to follow wise ways. Without You, even the most powerful nation becomes foolish.

Wisdom against Strife

Mockers stir up a city,
but wise men turn away anger.
Proverbs 29:8

P lenty of people can tear down, but building up a leader so that problems can be solved is a better solution, Lord. I recognize that. Yet I've found it easy enough to criticize or condemn a boss, a politician, or a church leader.

Instead of rushing to attack a person or a situation, I want to become a problem solver—one who turns to You for the right, peaceful solution. So move my heart far from anger and hurt, and give me Your peace to share with others. Help me not to mock them, but to turn aside anger and find a real solution. Then I know I'll be doing Your will.

GOD'S WISDOM

*But the wisdom that comes from heaven
is first of all pure.
It is also peace loving, gentle at all times,
and willing to yield to others.
It is full of mercy and good deeds.
It shows no partiality and is always sincere.*

JAMES 3:17 NLT

Your wisdom isn't brash or bossy, Lord, but pure and peaceful. It doesn't demand its own way or show prejudice. Often it seems the exact opposite of what passes for wisdom in this world. I've seen plenty of "wise" people who wouldn't fit Your description.

But I don't want to be like the world—I want to be like You, Jesus. So let me exemplify Your kind of peaceful wisdom, filled with mercy and goodness. Though many in this world may not admire it, I know You always will.

BLESSED WORK

Blessed are all who fear the LORD,
who walk in his ways.
You will eat the fruit of your labor;
blessings and prosperity will be yours.

PSALM 128:1–2

I don't like the idea of fearing You, Lord. I'd rather think of all the wonderful things You've done for me. But I have to admit I sometimes do the right thing because I don't want to suffer the ills You've promised to disobedient Christians. I can fear not obeying You; but because I love You, I want to do Your will.

If I do that, You promise I'll get more than I expected. Not only will I avoid trouble, I'll also find that my work isn't wasted. I'll be blessed by being able to keep the things You give me, and I'll enjoy their benefits.

Thank You, Lord, for this double blessing.

ILLICIT GAIN

Food gained by fraud tastes sweet to a man,
but he ends up with a mouth full of gravel.

PROVERBS 20:17

Lord, what a clear picture this verse gives me of Your attitude toward dishonest gain—I can almost taste the stones in my mouth! Clearly, a career as a thief is never in a Christian's future.

Today I probably won't be tempted to steal food. But I may feel pressured to take part in white-collar crime or some slick dishonesty. My coworkers may encourage me to take a "little extra" from the office or close my eyes to another's wrongdoing. But I know You won't okay such actions. They don't meet with Your perfect standard.

Keep me honest, Lord, no matter what the pressure. I don't want to end my days with only a mouthful of gravel to show for them.

GOD'S WORK

"He is the Rock; his work is perfect.
Everything he does is just and fair.
He is a faithful God who does no wrong;
how just and upright he is!"

DEUTERONOMY 32:4 NLT

Your work is wonderful, Lord. I've seen it in my own life with the change You've made in me because I trusted in You. I know that when You complete a job, it is well done.

Help me to follow in Your footsteps when it comes to work. Because I'm human, my labors won't be perfect, but they can be good if they're based on Your just, upright laws. As I try to be more like You, my work will improve and I'll be incredibly blessed.

Whatever I lay my hands to, I want to do it in You, Jesus, my Rock and my Redeemer.

WORTHY OF HIRE

The labourer is worthy of his hire.

LUKE 10:7 KJV

N o matter what kind of work I do, You provide me with a way to live, Lord. As you provided for those first-century Christians who went out to preach Your gospel, You want me to be supported. Even those who do Your work need a way to live.

But whether I labor in a factory or an office or preaching Your good news, You know all my needs. Whomever my work blesses, that person or group should help me have enough to live on. No one can live on nothing.

But I also want to do my best for those I work for. Let me be worthy of my hire by always giving an excellent effort. Then I will shine for Your kingdom.

Eternal Life

*"For God so loved the world that he gave his one and only Son,
that whoever believes in him shall not perish but have eternal life.
For God did not send his Son into the world to condemn the world,
but to save the world through him."*

John 3:16–17

I rejoice, Lord, that You loved people enough to sacrifice Your Son for us. Though our world thoroughly disobeyed You, You responded with forgiveness, inviting those who turn to You to share eternal life.

I can't fathom such self-sacrificing love, Lord, but I'm grateful You gave it to me. I'm also glad You offered it to the entire world, because I can't imagine where we'd be without the impact of those who have influenced society for You. Thank You, Jesus—help me to walk in faith and share Your forgiveness in a new way today.

Overcoming the World

Who is he that overcometh the world,
but he that believeth that Jesus is the Son of God?

1 John 5:5 KJV

When worldly temptations press in on me, I'm glad You gave me this promise, Jesus. It's hard to be in the world and not fall into its traps. But as I believe in You, who have overcome the world, I overcome it, too. I don't have to settle for giving in to the world's temptations and wickedness. You've given me the ability to fight back, in You—and to win through You.

I want to enjoy Your blessings for this life without being trapped in wrong thoughts or actions. Where You have overcome, I don't need to be defeated. Keep me faithful to You, Jesus, and my battle will be won.

THE WORLD'S END

I will punish the world for its evil,
the wicked for their sins.
I will put an end to the arrogance of the haughty
and will humble the pride of the ruthless.

ISAIAH 13:11

Those who hate You don't win forever, Lord. I'm glad You've given us this promise, so we know that whatever happens today isn't the end of the story. Though wicked people may seem to be on top now, either on this earth or in eternity they will learn differently. The truths You've shown me in scripture will be proved right, and the wicked will not win.

But it doesn't have to end that way if people recognize their sin today and turn from it. Use my witness to change lives on earth so some will have changed hearts—and changed eternities. Instead of settling for wickedness, let them live for You, Lord.

LIGHT OF THE WORLD

"You are the light of the world.
A city on a hill cannot be hidden."

MATTHEW 5:14

Y ou left a light in this wicked world, Lord—and it's me. That's a scary thought, because I don't like to think that without my witness Your work on earth could be less effective.

I know You call millions of people to Your work, and Your light cannot be hidden forever, but no one else is in my spot. Could my place be a critical one in the work You are doing?

I want to shine brightly for You, Jesus. You promise my light cannot be hidden, but it might burn faintly. I'd rather illuminate as much of my world as I can, Lord. Help me do just that.

ANXIETY CURE

*Cast all your anxiety on him
because he cares for you.*

1 PETER 5:7

What do I need to worry about when You are in charge of my life, Lord? Nothing in this world is greater than You.

But I do get concerned about the things I face. When money is running short or a relationship isn't going well, I can get so agitated that it's almost as if You weren't in my life anymore. I know that's not true, because You promised never to leave me—but I can certainly act as if it were so.

Remind me when worry attacks that I need only to cast every care on You. You will resolve everything better than I ever could. Thank You, Jesus, for loving me so much.

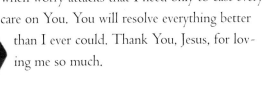

WORRY FOR TOMORROW

"So do not worry about tomorrow;
for tomorrow will care for itself.
Each day has enough trouble of its own."

MATTHEW 6:34 NASB

Some days have plenty of trouble, Lord, and it's easy for me to look ahead and wonder what the next day will bring. Then I start thinking about a week, a month, or a year ahead, and soon my whole life looks bleak. Once I start worrying, it's hard to stop.

Help me to remember that all You've given me is today—a single twenty-four-hour period to deal with. I need to focus on what I have before me in this day, not the days that lie beyond. And for this day I can ask for—and receive—all the help I need from You.

Help me, Jesus, with today's worries. Then tomorrow may not be a concern after all.

RIGHT WORDS

*"When you are arrested,
don't worry about what to say in your defense,
because you will be given
the right words at the right time.
For it won't be you doing the talking—
it will be the Spirit of your Father
speaking through you."*

MATTHEW 10:19–20 NLT

I may not be arrested, Lord, but there are still times when I have to stand up for You in front of people who have authority. Whenever someone confronts me about my faith, I need the right words and ideas to testify about You.

When I face such a situation, speak through me clearly. Empty my mind and heart of everything that's not from You. I want to let Your Spirit use my words to let others learn Your truth.

VALUED BY GOD

"And the very hairs on your head
are all numbered.
So don't be afraid;
you are more valuable to him than
a whole flock of sparrows."

LUKE 12:7 NLT

Sparrows aren't very important, Lord, yet You take care of even these small birds. Though some people may think them a nuisance, You know when each one falls.

Maybe it's not a huge compliment to be compared to sparrows, but I get Your message loud and clear. Everything about me, even down to how many hairs are on my head, is important to You. If You care about the birds, how much more important am I to You?

Thank You for having compassion even about the tiny things in my life. With that kind of concern, You're teaching me that I don't have to worry about a thing.

Scripture Index

Old Testament

Scripture Index

New Testament